Mel Bay's
BACK-UP BANJO

CD CONTENTS*

DISC 1

by Janet Davis

1. Introduction & Tuning (pg. 5) [:15]
2. Rhythm Exercises #1 (pg. 9) [:26]
3. Rhythm Exercises #2 (pg. 9) [:19]
4. Rhythm Exercises #3 (pg. 9) [:22]
5. Rhythm Exercises #4 (pg. 9) [:19]
6. Rhythm Exercises #5 (pg. 9) [:20]
7. Rhythm Exercises #6 (pg. 9) [:20]
8. Basic Vamping Pattern #1 (pg. 17) [:27]
9. Basic Vamping Pattern #2 (pg. 17) [:14]
10. Chord Progression (pg. 18) [:23]
11. Embellishment #1-3 (pg. 19) [:28]
12. Embellishment #4-9 (pg. 19) [:31]
13. Embellishment #10-12 (pg. 19) [:18]
14. Chord Prog. Pattern #2 (pg. 20) [:26]
15. Chord Prog. Pattern #10 & 2 (pg. 20) [:22]
16. Embellishment (pg. 21) [:48]
17. Basic Vamping Ptn. & Var. (pg. 22) [:43]
18. Embellishment Using Passing Tones (pg. 23) [:40]
19. Patterns #1-6 (pg. 24) [1:13]
20. Patterns #7-8 (pg. 25) [:27]
21. Patterns #1-4 (pg. 25) [:47]
22. Chord Progression #1 & 2 (pg. 26) [:44]
23. G Chord Fill-in Licks (pg. 28) [2:30]
24. C Chord Fill-in Licks (pg. 29) [1:13]
25. D Chord Fill-in Licks (pg. 29) [1:20]
26. Chord Prog. w/Fill-in Licks (pg. 28) [:46]
27. Fill-in Licks to G Chord (pg. 31) [:20]
28. Fill-in Licks to C Chord (pg. 31) [:25]
29. Songs Demonstrations (pg. 32) [:23]
30. Wabash Cannonball (pg. 33) [2:40]
31. John Hardy (pg. 39) [2:03]
32. Salt River (pg. 49) [2:55]
33. Scruggs-style Rolls (pg. 54) [:39]
34. Chord Prog. w/Forward Roll (pg. 55) [:35]
35. Chord Prog. w/Several Rolls (pg. 55) [:29]
36. Scruggs-style Deep Tones, Forward Roll, & Roll Variations (pg. 57) [1:09]
37. —Backward Roll & Back & Forward Roll (pg. 58) [1:14]
38. —Mixed Roll & Mixed Roll Var. (pg. 59) [:59]
39. —Forward-Reverse Roll (pg. 60) [1:10]
40. Var./Forward-Reverse Roll (pg. 61) [1:00]
41. Common G Chord Patterns (pg. 62) [:50]
42. Common C Chord Patterns (pg. 62) [:47]
43. Common D Chord Patterns (pg. 63) [1:13]
44. Chord Progression #1 (pg. 64) [:27]
45. Chord Progression #2 (pg. 64) [:23]
46. Passing Tones–G Chord (pg. 65) [:52]
47. Passing Tones–C Chord (pg. 65) [:45]
48. Passing Tones–D Chord (pg. 66) [:47]
49. Chord Progression (pg. 66) [:26]
50. Roll Patterns Using Passing Tones (pg. 67) [1:11]
51. Chord Progression #1 (pg. 68) [:26]
52. Chord Progression #2 (pg. 68) [:23]
53. Licks Using Passing Tones (pg. 69) [1:35]
54. Chord Progression #1 (pg. 71) [:26]
55. Chord Progression #2 (pg. 71) [:24]
56. Fill-in Licks Progression #1 (pg. 72) [:27]
57. Fill-in Licks Progression #2 (pg. 72) [:27]
58. Rhythmic Embellishment (pg. 73) [1:03]
59. Wabash Cannonball (pg. 75) [:26]
60. John Hardy (pg. 76) [:30]

This book is available either by itself or packaged with a companion audio and/or video recording. If you have purchased the book only, you may wish to purchase the recordings separately. The publisher strongly recommends using a recording along with the text to assure accuracy of interpretation and make learning easier and more enjoyable.

DISC 2

1. Scruggs-style–Up-the Neck & Forward Roll (pg. 86) [:46]
2. Adding Color to Forward Roll (pg. 87) [:59]
3. Chord Progression #1 (pg. 87) [:32]
4. Syncopated Forward Roll (pg. 88) [:49]
5. Chord Progression #2 (pg. 88) [:25]
6. Backward Roll (pg. 89) [:56]
7. Chord Progression #3 (pg. 89) [:33]
8. The Mixed Roll (pg. 90) [:48]
9. Chord Progression #4 (pg. 90) [:24]
10. The Forward-Reverse Roll (pg. 91) [:48]
11. Chord Progression Ptns 1-4 (pg. 91) [:55]
12. Chord Progression #5 (pg. 92) [:40]
13. Chord Progression #6 (pg. 92) [:28]
14. Up the Neck Fill-in Licks (pg. 93) [:29]
15. F Position Licks #1-4 (pg. 94) [:46]
16. D Position Licks #5-8 (pg. 94) [:49]
17. Barre Position Licks #9-14 (pg. 95) [1:14]
18. Licks Using Single Strings #15-20 (pg. 96) [1:06]
19. Licks Using Single Strings #21-25 (pg. 97) [1:18]
20. Up-the-Neck Licks (for Specific Chords) –G Chord Licks #26-33 (pg. 98) [1:02]
21. –C Chord Licks #34-37 (pg. 98) [:31]
22. –D Chord Licks #38-41 (pg. 98) [:32]
23. Chord Progression #1 (pg. 99) [:27]
24. Chord Progression #2 (pg. 99) [:22]
25. Wabash Cannonball (pg. 101) [2:39]
26. John Hardy (pg. 107) [1:52]
27. Endings: Vocal (pg. 120) [1:06]
28. Endings: Instrumental (pg. 120) [:32]
29. Jesse James (pg. 135) [3:20]
30. Battle Hymn of the Republic (pg. 152) [1:15]
31. Sally Goodin' (pg. 185) [1:41]
32. Blackberry Blossom (pg. 193) [3:16]
33. Back-up for Slow Songs #1-2 (pg. 204) [:27]
34. Back-up for Slow Songs #3-9 (pg. 205) [1:30]
35. Chord Progression (pg. 206) [:29]
36. Wabash Cannonball (pg. 207) [1:08]
37. Waltz Time Patterns #1-3 (pg. 213) [:36]
38. Roll Patterns (pg. 214) [1:16]
39. Fill-in Licks #1-4 (pg. 215) [1:23]
40. Fill-in Licks #5-8 (pg. 216) [1:14]
41. Chord Progression #1 (pg. 217) [:24]
42. Chord Progression #2 (pg. 217) [:24]
43. Chord Progression #3 (pg. 218) [:26]
44. All the Good Times Are Past (pg. 219) [4:20]

1 2 3 4 5 6 7 8 9 0

Visit us on the Web at www.melbay.com — E-mail us at email@melbay.com

TABLE OF CONTENTS

FOREWORD

The primary aim of this book is to present, explain, and exemplify the basic techniques commonly used on the five string banjo to accompany vocalists and/or instrumentalists. "BACK-UP" is simply another term for "ACCOMPANIMENT".

This book is designed so that a beginning student of back-up can become accomplished at playing back-up for many different songs, using the techniques commonly used by many professional banjo players. The basic outline of the book separates the various back-up techniques into categories. These are determined by the tempo of the song being played, by the lead instrument being accompanied, and by the area of the fingerboard in which the chords are being played. The first section of the book deals with general back-up techniques, which can be used as back-up for songs played at ANY tempo (speed), and which can be used as back-up for ANY lead instrument playing the melody. As the book progresses, each style of back-up becomes more specialized. Each section of the book is also designed so that it first discusses the basic techniques and uses for a particular style of back-up, and then goes into some of the means for adding polish to that style of back-up.

The guidelines and the back-up patterns offered throughout this book are based upon common practice among professional banjo players, and will, hopefully, provide you with the tools for playing effective back-up for many different songs.

Happy Pickin'

Janet Davis

INTRODUCTION
What Is Back-Up?

A banjo player normally plays accompaniment at least 75% of the time when he is playing with a band or with another musician, or when he is singing, while only about 25% of his effort involves playing the melody of the song. Therefore, an important aspect of playing the banjo is the art of playing back-up. "BACK-UP" is simply another term for "ACCOMPANIMENT".

Back-up played on the banjo consists essentially of a combination of two elements: CHORDS & RHYTHM. For most styles of back-up, the left hand works from chord positions, while the right hand plays specific fingering patterns. The same patterns can be used as back-up for many different songs. Which patterns are used for a specific song will be determined primarily by the tempo of the song, and by which instrument is playing the melody.

The art of playing back-up on the banjo can, in many respects, be compared to the art of building a structure with a set of blocks of various shapes and sizes. The same set of blocks can be used to build many different structures. All of the blocks might be used for one type of building, whereas only a few blocks of a specific shape might be required for another building. Certain blocks might be more useful for foundation purposes (i.e. for support), while other blocks might serve more ornamental functions. Each style of back-up contains a definite set of patterns which can be used over and over as back-up for many different songs. How the patterns are used, where they are placed in the context of the songs, when embellishment techniques are used,--all of these things work together to determine the overall effectiveness of the back-up for a specific song.

DEFINITIONS

1. ACCENT: stress or play louder, (but not longer).

2. BACK-UP: Accompaniment

3. BREAK: When an instrument plays the melody to a song. (i.e. the back-up played on the banjo for a mandolin "break" may differ from that played for a dobro "break" in the same song.)

4. CHORD PROGRESSION: series of chords. Songs are built upon chord progressions.

5. COMMON PRACTICE: the usual way something is played.

6. DOWN THE NECK: toward the tuning machinery; the lower fret numbers are located "down-the-neck"; down = lower in pitch.

7. EMBELLISH: ornament; to add interest.

8. INSTRUMENTAL: a song which does NOT include singing; the melody is played only by the instruments.

9. LINK: fill-in lick(s) used to connect one break (or verse) with the next break in a song.

10. LEAD: melody or tune to the song.

11. MEASURE: the notes occurring between two bar lines in music or tablature constitute one measure. Usually one roll pattern equals one measure of music.

12. PICK UP NOTES: the notes used to begin a song; normally these notes are played only by the lead instrument to introduce the song, and the back-up does not play along with them; normally the pick-up notes do not form a complete measure of music, and therefore are used only at the beginning of the song.

13. TEMPO: speed or pace at which a song is played.

14. UP-THE-NECK: toward the head of the banjo, away from the peghead; the higher the fret number, the higher the tone sounds; up-the-neck = higher in pitch = higher fret number.

15. VERSE; REFRAIN (chorus): many songs, and especially those which have words, are comprised of two parts . . . the verse and the refrain (also called the chorus). Normally the verse uses different words each time it is sung, while the refrain uses the same words each time it is sung. Also, the chorus may follow each verse, or it may be sung after several verses have already been sung. The refrain may use the same tune as the verse, or it may be a different tune. Normally these terms will be used with reference to vocals.

16. VOCAL: a song which includes singing; a singing song.

GENERAL GUIDELINES
for Effective Back-Up

The following list of general guidelines for playing effective back-up are based upon common practice, and are founded upon the principles of providing support for and avoiding competition with the lead instrument.

1. PLAY QUIETLY . . . Stay in the background. If playing into a microphone, step back from it when playing back-up, (but play right into it when playing the lead(melody). It is easy to have so much fun playing back-up that you forget that you are not supposed to be the center of attention. However, you may receive a few dirty looks, instead of looks of admiration. Your overall objective should be to COMPLIMENT the lead instrument, not compete with it.

2. LISTEN TO THE LEAD INSTRUMENT AND STRIVE FOR BALANCE . . . a general rule is: play on the higher tones of the banjo, (up-the-neck), when the lead instrument is playing the deep tones; play with the deeper tones of the banjo (near the peghead), when the lead is playing higher pitched tones, (i.e. if the lead instrument is the fiddle or the mandolin).

3. RIGHT HAND POSITION IS IMPORTANT! . . . when the left hand is playing up-the-neck on the higher pitched tones of the banjo, the right hand should be positioned close to the fingerboard in the "Y" Position, (see diagram below). When playing with the deeper tones of the banjo, the right hand should pick the strings near the bridge in the "X" Position. Right hand positioning is one method the banjo player uses to add expression to the overall effect of the song.

4. LISTEN TO THE TEMPO OF THE SONG . . . find a back-up rhythm pattern (or style) that will fit that particular tempo. (Generally, you will be safe if you "Vamp" chords high on the fingerboard while you are getting a "feeling" for the song. See p. 16).

5. FILL IN THE GAPS . . . Generally the banjo should come forward (play louder) and play fill-in licks during the pauses in the melody line, (i.e. when the vocalist takes a breath, or between verses . . . see p. 27).

6. LISTEN TO THE TOTAL EFFECT OF THE SONG . . . if other instruments are also playing back-up, try to do something that they aren't doing. Step back if another instrument is taking the dominant role in the back-up, and you find you are competing. (Often, the instruments will take turns as the dominant back-up instrument . . . i.e. the banjo may be the active back-up instrument for the first verse, and the mandolin may dominate the back-up for the next verse to the song.)

7. EFFECTIVE BACK-UP INVOLVES KNOWING AND PLAYING CHORDS! (p. 10) Also, the frequent use of passing tones greatly enhances the overall effectiveness of the song. (see p. 23)

EXPLANATION OF TABLATURE AND RHYTHM

I. The <u>tablature</u> used in this book is fairly standard:

The <u>five</u> <u>lines</u> represent the <u>five</u> <u>strings</u>; the top line is the first string, and the bottom line is the 5th string, (the short string).

The <u>number</u> tells you which <u>fret</u> to push down with your left hand. (O means open--don't push the string down with the left hand when picking it with the right hand).

T, I, M = are <u>fingering</u> <u>indications</u> for the <u>right hand</u>. <u>M</u> means pick the string with the middle finger; <u>I</u> means index finger; <u>T</u> means thumb.

t, i, m, r, p = <u>Left</u> <u>hand</u> <u>fingering</u>: t=thumb; i=index; m=middle; r=ring; p=pinky.

H, P, Sl, Ch = are left hand techniques used for sounding the strings with the <u>left hand</u>; (the right hand picks the note preceding them)

<u>H</u> means to <u>hammer</u> the fret indicated, by pushing down the string with the left finger, hard enough to sound the tone.

<u>P</u> means to <u>pull off</u> of the string from the fret <u>before</u> the one to be sounded by the pull off, therefore sounding the tone indicated above the <u>P</u>.

<u>SL</u> means to sound the tone by <u>sliding</u> to the fret number above the Sl with the left finger(s) from the number before it.

<u>Ch</u> means to <u>bend</u> the string with the left finger, (do not pick the string with the right hand, just bend it). (<u>Ch</u>=<u>choke</u>)

> OR- means to stress or <u>accent</u> this tone...play it louder.

<u>NOTE</u>: For more complete explanations of the above indications, refer to a beginning banjo book.

II. The <u>rhythm</u> used in this book is also standard notation:

Each measure consists of 4 counts (or eight $\frac{1}{2}$ counts).
The measures are divided by bar lines.

The <u>stems</u> under the notes (or numbers) tell you how long to let the notes ring:

eighth note = $\frac{1}{2}$ count. (Eighth notes are written alone, ♪ , in pairs, ♫ , or in fours, ♬ .)

quarter note = 1 count. (one quarter note=two eighth notes: ♩ = ♫)
(hold the ♩ tone for the duration of ♫)

sixteenth note = $\frac{1}{4}$ count. (play two sixteenth notes in the same amount of time you play one eighth note. ♬ = ♪)

eighth rest = $\frac{1}{2}$ count. (rest=silence for the indicated duration.)

quarter rest=1 count.

Syncopation commonly used in back-up. short-long = hold the quarter note for the same duration it takes to play two eighth notes.

long-short. (A dotted note is held $1\frac{1}{2}$ times the normal value of the note... i.e. ♩. = $1\frac{1}{2}$ counts.)

‖: or :‖ repeat sign. (play again before continuing.)
Return to the previous ‖: if there is one; otherwise, return to the beginning and repeat the section.

RHYTHM

Rhythm is an essential and integral component of back-up. If you have difficulty reading rhythm and playing it, the following exercises may help.

When playing through each exercise:
1. Tap your foot: DOWN-UP-DOWN-UP... with an <u>even</u> rhythm (over & over). (Don't pause at the bar line.)
2. Pick the open 3rd string for each note, (or simply tap the head of your banjo). The point of the exercise is to play rhythm only.
3. Count out loud and play the notes with the <u>correct</u> count. (Remember: a rest means silence.)
   NOTE: You MUST keep your rhythm EVEN, whether counting or tapping you foot, or both.

EXERCISES: (watch the stems on the notes!)

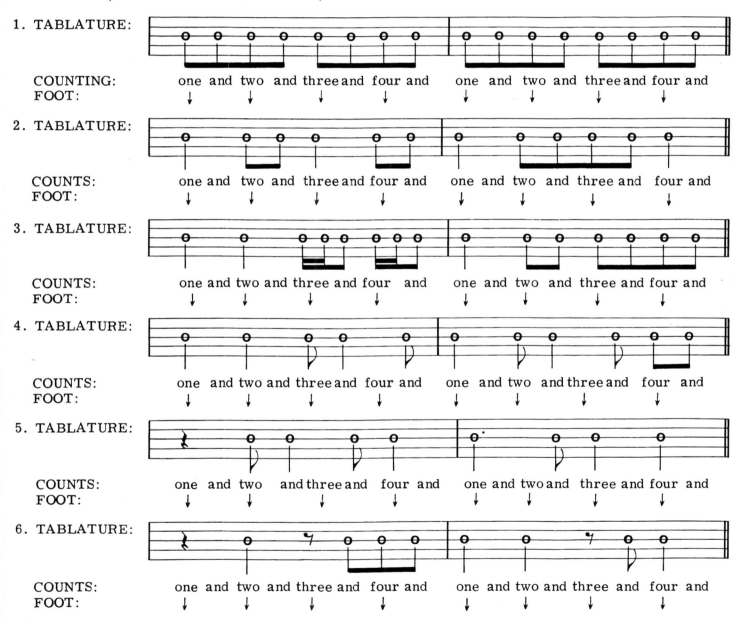

* #4, #5, & #6 include syncopated rhythm patterns, (where the accent falls on the up beat instead of on the down beat.)

CHORDS

When playing back-up on the banjo, the left hand works almost entirely from chord positions. For this reason, an essential step to learning to play back-up is learning to play chords. It is not necessary to learn 25 different chord positions in order to play back-up. The banjo doesn't work that way. Instead, it works from chord PATTERNS. To begin to play back-up, you need to learn only three chord position patterns, and you will be able to play back-up for any major chord in any area of the fingerboard. (All of the other chords, i.e. minor, diminished, augmented, seventh, etc. can be found and learned in relation to these three positions.) Each chord pattern involves only the first four strings of the banjo. (Unless the 5th string is a chord tone of the chord being played, it is generally avoided in back-up.) <u>THE CHORD NAME IS DETERMINED BY WHERE THE LEFT HAND HOLDS THE CHORD PATTERN ON THE FINGERBOARD.</u> For example: an F chord is played with the "F" Position pattern on the first three frets of the banjo. By moving this pattern two frets higher, to the third, fourth, and fifth frets, a G chord will be played with the "F" Position pattern.

THE MAJOR CHORD PATTERNS:

The following left hand patterns can be used to play any MAJOR CHORD:

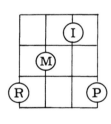
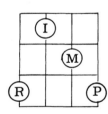
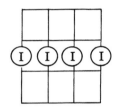

"F" Position   "D" Position   "Barre" Position
(Lay the index finger across all 4 strings)

The Chord Chart on the following page demonstrates how each chord pattern can be moved up the fingerboard to play any major chord. Notice that the chord names change in alphabetical order as each pattern travels up the neck. (The musical alphabet = A-G, repeated over and over.) This should help you locate specific chords in each position, when you don't have a chord chart. Because back-up licks work from these chord positions, be careful to use the correct left hand fingers to form each chord position.

NOTE: Complete chord charts are located in the back of this book! See pages 234-238.

MOVEABLE CHORD POSITION CHART
MAJOR CHORDS

*The number by each individual diagram tells you what fret the chord starts on.
*Use the correct left hand fingering to form each chord position.
  (I=index; M=middle; R=ring; P=pinky)

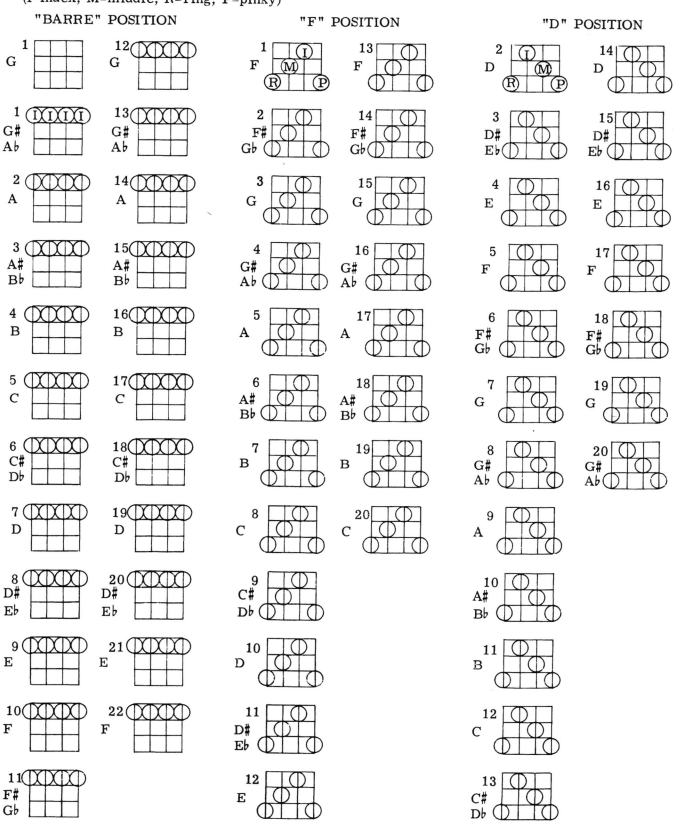

11

EXERCISES

If you are not already adept at playing chords all over the fingerboard, work first with the G, C, and D chords. Many traditional bluegrass songs use these chords, and all of the other major chords can be learned in relation to the location of these chords. Practice the following exercises until you are able to change from one chord position to another, smoothly and without hesitation. Learn the names of the chords as you play their positions. Hold full chord positions with the left hand.

Practice changing from G to C to D to G using only one moveable chord pattern. Slide the left fingers along the strings from one position to the next.

Practice changing from G to C to D to G in one area of the fingerboard.

Practice changing from the "F" position to the "D" position of each chord:

LOCATING CHORDS WITHOUT A CHART
(COMPLETE CHORD CHARTS ARE LOCATED IN THE BACK OF THIS BOOK)

1. Notice on p.11, that the chord names change in alphabetical order as each chord position pattern is moved up the fingerboard. (The musical alphabet = A through G, repeated over and over.) Notice that B is located next to C, and also that E is next to F, but that all other letters are separated by a fret. (The frets in between work like the black keys on a piano.) To locate a specific chord without a chord chart, you can start with one of the chord position patterns, such as the "F" Position F chord, and move it up the fingerboard until you arrive at the desired chord alphabetically. If you know all of the positions for the G, C, and D chords, you can also find the other chords in relation to these chords. For example, the E chord is always located two frets higher (in pitch) than the D chord.

2. ♯ means to "sharp" or raise (in pitch) one fret. Therefore, any chord with this symbol following the letter will be located one fret above the position of the chord letter. i.e. G♯ is located one fret position above the G chord.

3. ♭ means to "flat" or lower (in pitch) one fret. Therefore, any chord with this symbol following the letter will be located one fret lower than the regular position for this chord. i.e. B♭ is located one fret lower (in pitch) than B.

4. Minor chords, diminished chords, and augmented chords can be located by first locating normal major chord position for the desired chord. Each of these chords requires altering a tone of the major chord. (See charts pp. 234-238 for more explanation.) The following diagrams demonstate how these chords can be located from the major chord position.

	MAJOR	MINOR	DIMINISHED	AUGMENTED	(dominant) SEVENTH
"F" POSITION:	(chord diagram)	(chord diagram)	(chord diagram)	(chord diagram)	(chord diagram)
"D" POSITION:	(chord diagram)	(chord diagram)	(chord diagram)	(chord diagram)	(chord diagram)
"BARRE" POSITION:	(chord diagram)	(chord diagram)	(chord diagram)	(chord diagram)	(chord diagram)

NOTE: Barre the left index finger across the strings, when it is indicated on more than one string in a chord position.

5. A number following a chord symbol, (i.e. G7 = dominant 7th chord) means that an extra tone is added to the chord. (The major chord can also be substituted for chords of this nature.)

BASIC BACK-UP TECHNIQUES

The following section will cover various back-up techniques that can be used for any type of lead---vocal, or instrumental, and for songs played at any tempo---fast or slow. These techniques will also provide the foundation for the other styles of back-up discussed in this book.

VAMPING

VAMPING is a commonly used back-up technique which involves playing rhythm and chords. This technique can be used as back-up for any song, to accompany any lead instrument or vocalist. It can be used as the only back-up technique throughout an entire song, or it can be combined with other styles of back-up. The vamping technique can be used with any chord, or with every chord in a song. You can't go wrong using the vamping technique as a style of back-up. Although vamping is often treated as a beginning back-up technique, its' use is by no means limited to beginners. Many great back-up artists use this technique frequently! The vamping style of back-up is particularly effective for breakdowns and for other fast instrumentals, such as "Foggy Mountain Breakdown", "Earl's Breakdown", and "Flinthill Special". It is also effective for up-tempo vocals such as "Footprints In the Snow" and "Salty Dog", as well as for slower paced songs such as "I Wonder Where You Are Tonight". Jazz tunes are frequently supported by vamping. The vamping style of back-up is often used as the primary style of accompaniment for guitar and dobro lead breaks.

"Vamping" is effective ONLY if it is played correctly. It is NOT simply picking chords to the rhythm of a song. Vamping also involves DAMPENING the strings with the left hand, after each chord is plucked with the right fingers.

STEP 1: Hold a chord position with the left hand.
(Hold the full position--all four strings.)

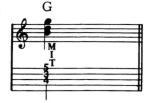

STEP 2: Pick the 1st, 2nd, & 3rd strings with M, I, & T of the right hand (simultaneously).* This should sound the chord.

STEP 3: Now, partially release the pressure on the strings with the left hand. This should STOP the tones from sustaining. DON'T LET THE CHORD RING AFTER THE RIGHT HAND PLAYS IT. Release the pressure of the left fingers, but DO NOT lift the fingers from the strings. The left fingers deaden the sound in this manner. (The 5th string is not used with this technique.)

NOTE: When chording up-the-neck, on the higher pitched tones of the banjo, the right hand should pick the strings in the area of the banjo where the fingerboard joins the head, well away from the bridge, ("Y" position).

*The early style of vamping involved picking only the first two strings with the right hand. The third string was added sometime later, giving the back-up a fuller sound, and providing stronger harmonic support for the lead instrument.

BASIC VAMPING PATTERNS

The following patterns can be used as back-up patterns for any song. EACH PATTERN CAN BE USED WHILE HOLDING ANY CHORD WITH THE LEFT HAND. The same pattern can be used as back-up throughout an entire song, or it can be used in combination with other patterns. (One pattern = one measure of music or tablature.)

1. The following pattern plays on every beat or pulse. Dampen the tones with the left hand each time the right hand picks the strings.

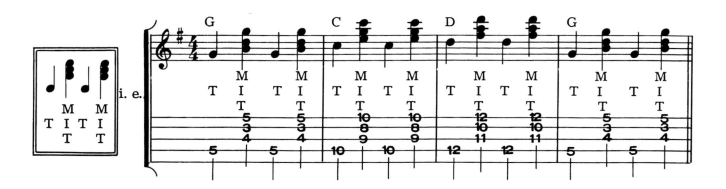

2. The most common right hand rhythmic pattern using the vamping technique is played as follows: (If this rhythm is difficult for you to "feel", continue making the picking motion with your right thumb as in #1 above, but don't actually pick the string. Only beats 2 and 4 should be sounded.)

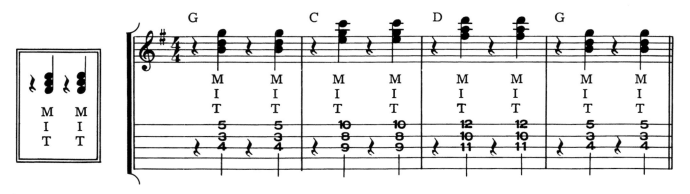

SUGGESTION: Practice vamping the chords to several of the songs for which you have the tablature. (Play two vamps per measure using pattern #2 above. This pattern can be used with any kind of music -- bluegrass, folk songs, pop songs, etc.)

NOTE: If a song calls for two different chords in the same measure of music, generally, the left hand holds the first chord for the first half (two beats) of the measure, and the second for the second half of the measure.

When learning back-up, it is helpful to apply each newly acquired technique to a chord progression, to see how it fits in the context of a song. The technique or pattern should then be easy to use for other chords in other songs. The following chord progression is very common to many tunes. When played twice, it is equal to one complete verse for a song: G(two measures) --C(two measures)--D(two measures)--G(two measures). The songs, "Blueridge Cabin Home", "Prisoner's Song", "Ride Em Down Easy", "Red Apple Rag", "Huckleberry Hornpipe", and "We'll Meet Again Sweetheart" use this same chord progression. The following arrangements using the basic vamping patterns can be used as back-up for any of the above mentioned songs.

CHORD PROGRESSION

Using vamping pattern #1 for each measure

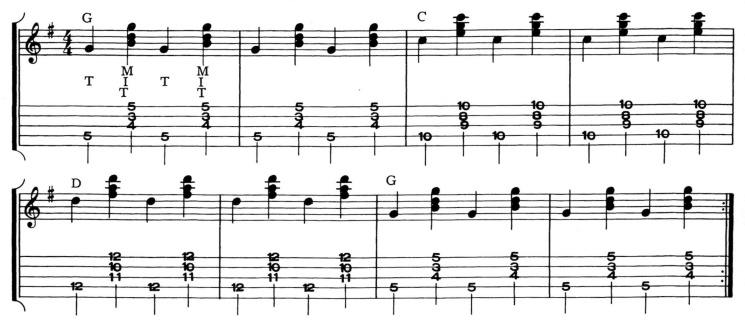

NOTE: Once you can play through the above progression smoothly, substitute vamping pattern #2 for each measure, (2 vamps per measure).

NOTE: Practice the above progression using different positions of the same chords with the left hand. For example, hold the "D" Position for each chord. Also, play through the progression while holding chord positions in one area of the fingerboard. (The right hand pattern and the chord names will remain the same.)

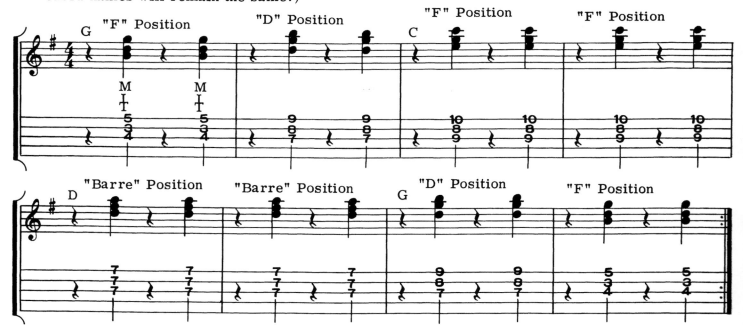

RHYTHMIC EMBELLISHMENT USING
VAMPING PATTERN VARIATIONS

The following back-up patterns can be played with the right hand while holding ANY chord position with the left hand. (The left hand should hold full chord positions--all four strings.) Each pattern can be used as back-up for an entire song, or it can be used to embellish the back-up. (In each of the syncopated patterns, the rest, (𝄽), is substituted for the 4th string tone. If the rhythm of these patterns causes you any difficulty, simply pick the 4th string instead of pausing for the rest, (or you might make the picking motion with your right thumb, without actually sounding the string.)

EACH PATTERN CAN BE USED FOR ANY CHORD:

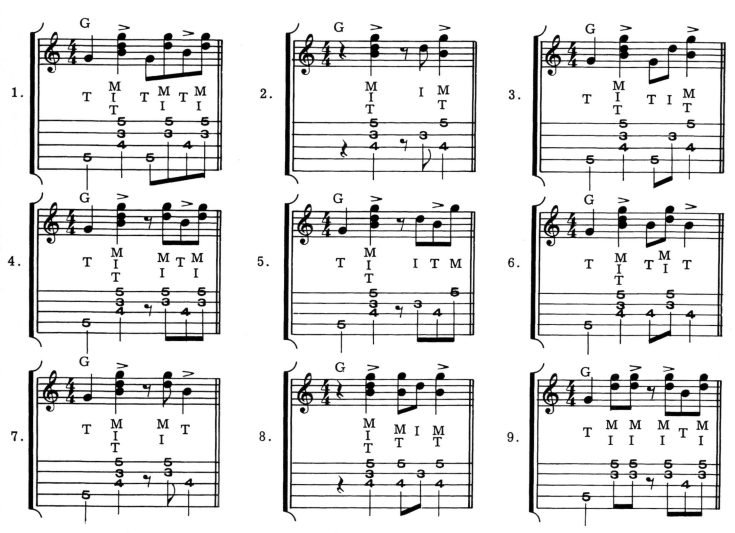

The following patterns are two of the most commonly used variations of the basic vamping pattern, when the left hand is playing a chord in the "F" Position. (All of the previous patterns can be used for any chord in any position.)

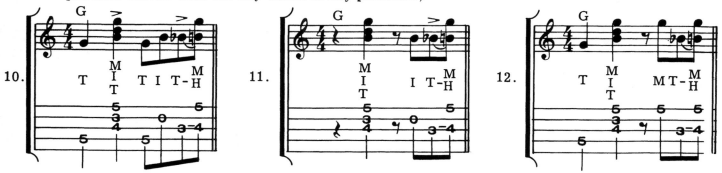

19

CHORD PROGRESSION
(USING VARIATION PATTERN #2)

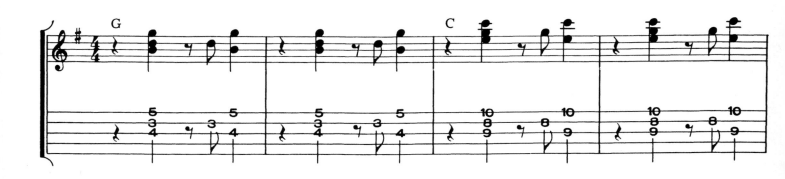

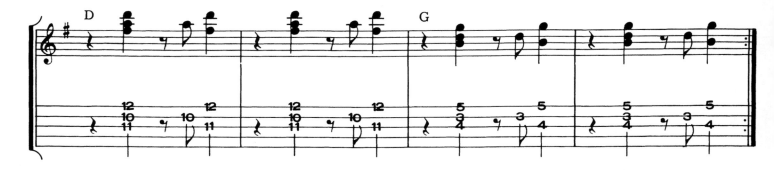

CHORD PROGRESSION
(USING VARIATION PATTERNS #10 & #2)

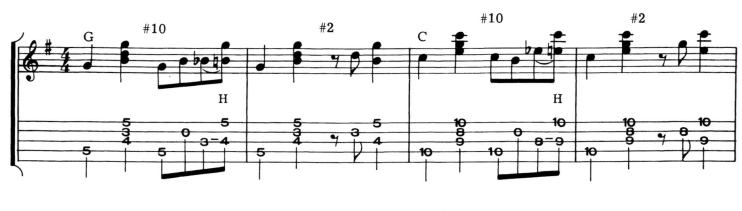

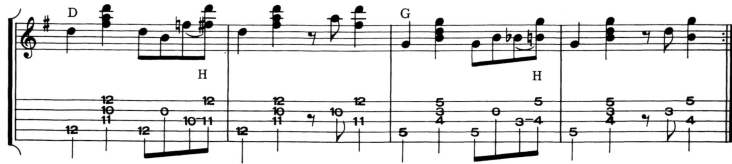

NOTE: Substitute each of the variation patterns from the preceding page for those used in the above chord progressions. Work with the patterns one at a time, until you are very familiar with each of them. Then try using several of the patterns in the same chord progression.

EMBELLISHMENT USING
TWO POSITIONS OF THE SAME CHORD

It is often effective to change from one position of a chord to the next closest position of the same chord with the left hand, (i.e. from the "F" position to the "D" position of the chord.) This adds a rhythmic bounce to the back-up and is often used to emphasize a particular area of a song.

1. To divide each of the vamping patterns between two positions of the same chord, simply play the first half of the pattern, (♩ 𝄂 or 𝄽 𝄂) in the lower position of the chord, (i.e. "F" Position), and move to the next position for the last half (two beats) of the pattern. For example:

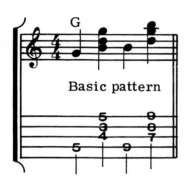

Basic pattern

Pattern #2

Pattern #6

2. You can also syncopate the rhythm between the two chord positions. The following pattern can be used for any chord, and is frequently used as back-up for the A chord when a song is played in the key of G, (i.e. "Salty Dog", "Dear Old Dixie", "Homestead On The Farm").

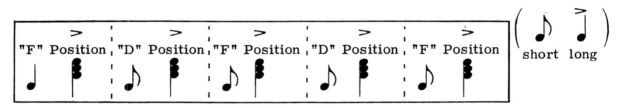

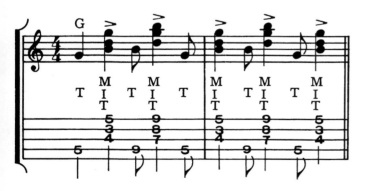

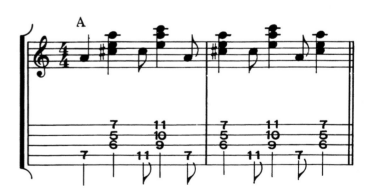

NOTE: The above embellishing techniques can also be applied when playing two different chords (as opposed to two different positions of the same chord).

EMBELLISHMENT
USING THE SLIDE

Sliding the left hand from one chord position to the next, and sounding the tones of the slide as the left hand moves along the strings, is one of the most commonly used embellishing techniques with the vamping style * of back-up. The slide can be used to lead the ear of the listener away from a chord, into a new chord, or it can be used primarily to accentuate a specific chord by sliding in and out of the chord position. The slide can be used to embellish any of the vamping patterns on the preceding pages. (The left hand should not dampen the tone picked just before the slide.) To emphasize the slide, the right hand should be positioned over the area of the banjo where the fingerboard joins the head, ("Y" Position).
FOR EXAMPLE:

THE BASIC VAMPING PATTERN:

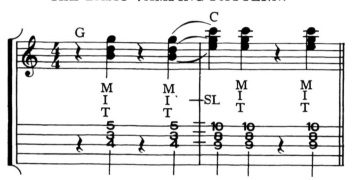 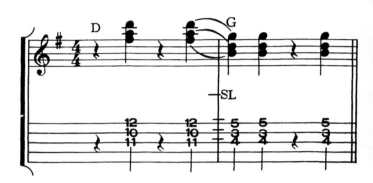

VAMPING VARIATION: This pattern is commonly used to change chords in the vamping style of back-up.

 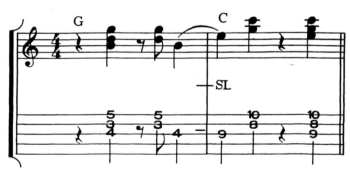

This pattern is also frequently used to move from the "F" Position to the "D" Position, (or vice versa,) of the <u>same</u> chord.

"F" Position to "D" Position

"D" Postion to "F" Position

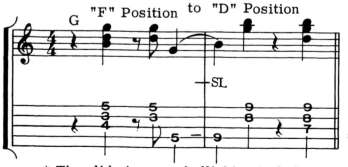 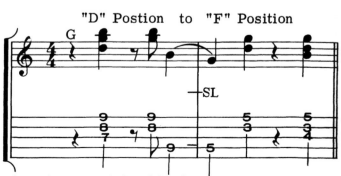

* The slide is an embellishing technique used with almost every style of back-up.

EMBELLISHMENT USING PASSING TONES

An important function of back-up played in any style, is that of giving the song a sense of harmonic direction. One way this can be accomplished is by playing passing tones to connect the tones of the chords. Passing tones can be used to lead the ear of the listener into new chords, or they can be used to embellish the back-up by connecting chord tones of the same chord. Passing tones can be played as single tones, or they can be played as passing chords. The following definitions should explain this:

CHORD TONES: (also called harmonic tones): the notes belonging to a specific chord. (Non-harmonic tones are any notes not belonging to that specific chord.) To locate chord tones, play the chord; those tones are the chord tones.

PASSING TONES: (a type of non-harmonic tone): the tones located between two chord tones in a scale line, (either diatonic or chromatic). The passing tones are used to lead the music from one chord tone to the next chord tone.

To see the effect of passing tones, play a chord, (any chord), on your banjo. Then move one of your left fingers up or down the fingerboard, one (or two) frets. This alters the chord, and should give you the feeling that the music is going somewhere else. (A useful guideline is to go to the closest position of the new chord.)
For example:

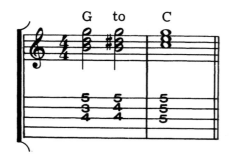 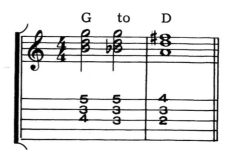

The following examples use passing tones to change from one chord to another chord. Notice that the passing tones are played while the song is on the first chord, for they lead the ear to the new chord. Each of these examples is actually a fingerboard pattern that can be applied to any chord when it is changing to a chord an equivalent fingerboard distance away, (& is separated by the same number of letters alphabetically). i.e. The patterns used to change from G to C can be used to change from A to D by playing each of the notes two frets higher.

"WALKING" THE 4th STRING:

Pattern for chord positions 5 frets apart. (Measure distance on 4th string.)

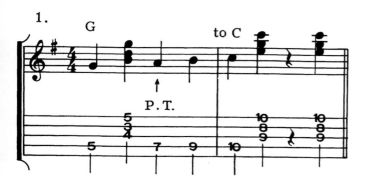 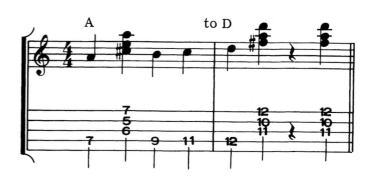

Pattern #1 in reverse (down the fingerboard)

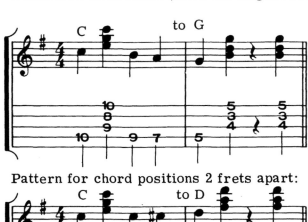

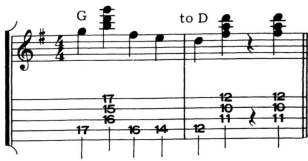

Pattern for chord positions 2 frets apart:

2.

Pattern #2 in reverse

Pattern for chord positions 3 frets apart:

3.

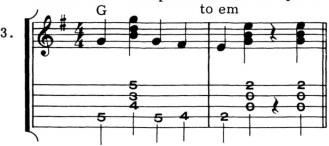

Variation of pattern #1*

4.

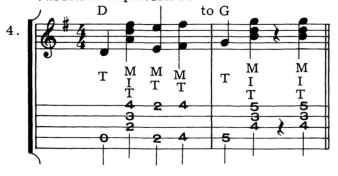

Pattern for chord positions 7 frets apart.

5.

* A bounce can be added to the back-up by playing the passing tones on both the 4th and 1st strings (same frets). All of the above examples can (and are frequently) played in this manner. (i.e. see #4 and #5)

6.

** The rhythm of each pattern can also be varied. i.e.:

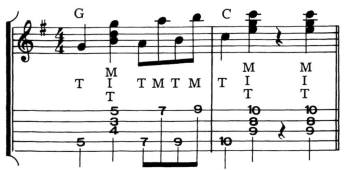

PASSING TONES FROM THE "D" POSITION OF THE CHORD:
(Hold the "D" position of the first chord in each pattern below; then move the left fingers as required to play the notes.)

7.
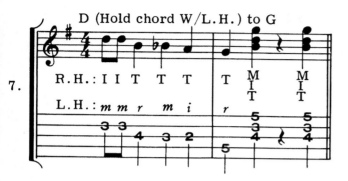
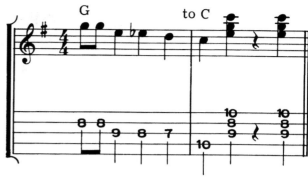

The following pattern uses passing tones to embellish the (same) chord:

8.
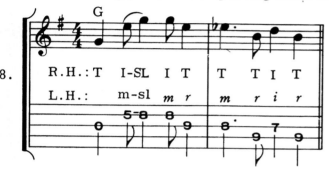

PASSING CHORDS:
Each of the following examples is a frequently used back-up pattern, which involves passing through several chords when changing from one chord in a song to another chord. (i.e. The refrain of many songs played in the Key of G, begins on the C chord. The following examples for going from G to C are frequently used to link the last chord of the verse (G) with the first chord of the refrain (C).)

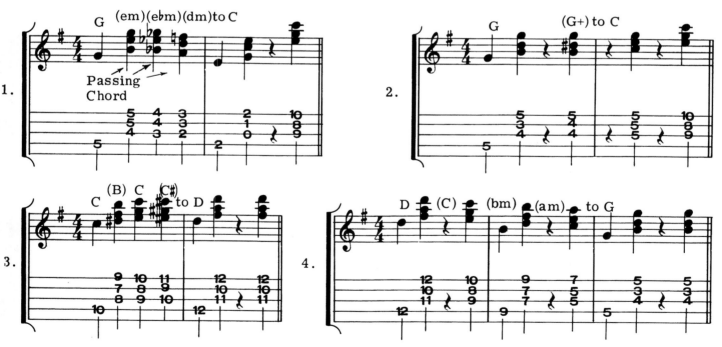

NOTE: To cover all of the possibilities for using passing tones would require another book. All of the above examples are commonly used to change chords in back-up. Experiment with various chords, and see what you can come up with on your banjo.

CHORD PROGRESSION
(USING PASSING TONES)

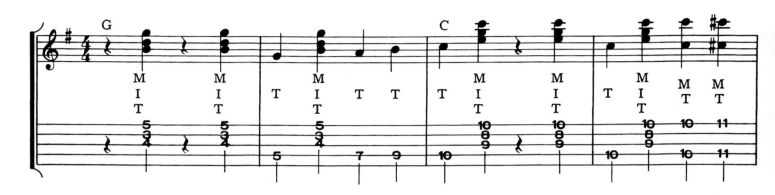

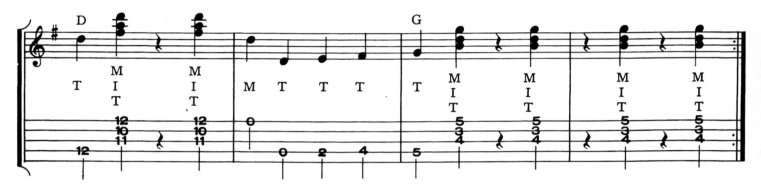

CHORD PROGRESSION
(USING PASSING CHORDS)

* BR = brush across all four strings with your right index and/or middle finger(s) (toward your face).
(OR - you can pick the 1st three strings with M, I, and T and vamp the chords.)

EMBELLISHMENT
FILL-IN LICKS
(LINKS)

One of the most important embellishing techniques used in all styles of back-up involves playing fill-in licks during the cadences of a song. These licks are the punctuation of the accompaniment. Fill-in licks are used in back-up primarily for the following reasons:

1. To fill in the pauses between the melody lines in a song. (i.e. when the singer takes a breath, a fill-in lick is normally played by the banjo.)
2. To emphasize the close of a lead break. (The fill-in lick acts as a period or as an exclamation mark.)
3. As a LINK: i.e. a.) to connect the verse with the refrain (chorus);
    b.) to connect the refrain with the next verse;
    c.) to connect the end of the refrain with an instrumental lead break;
    d.) to connect two instrumental breaks;
    e.) to connect the end of an instrumental break with the beginning of a verse in a singing song. (Often an extra lick - or two-is required to signal the vocalist to start singing.)

NOTE: Fill-in licks are usually played LOUDER than the rest of the back-up played by the banjo.

Although any lick played on the banjo can be used as a fill-in lick, certain licks have become fairly standard for use as fill-in licks for the G, C, and D chords. These licks are used ONLY for specific chords, and unlike many back-up licks, they are NOT patterns which can be applied to any chord. (This is primarily because these licks employ open strings.) Notice that the licks on the following pages are played between the open position and the 5th fret of the fingerboard. These licks are especially effective when played with vamping and with up-the-neck back-up, for they will really stand out.

NOTE: Play each lick ONLY for the corresponding chord in the song. (Use a G lick for a G chord.)

NOTE: Any two of the following licks can be combined. (For longer pauses, simply add more licks for the same chord.)

NOTE: The same lick can be used for every pause in a song, if desired. Also, the same lick can be played twice in a row, when more than one fill-in lick is required for a single pause. The PLACEMENT of the licks in the back-up is more important to the overall effect, than which lick is used to fill-in the pause.

The following pages contain examples of some very popular fill-in licks used in back-up. However, many other licks can also be used. Once you become familiar with these licks and are able to use them with ease, try using some of the licks you play in lead breaks for these same chords as fill-in licks when you are playing back-up.

G CHORD FILL-IN LICKS

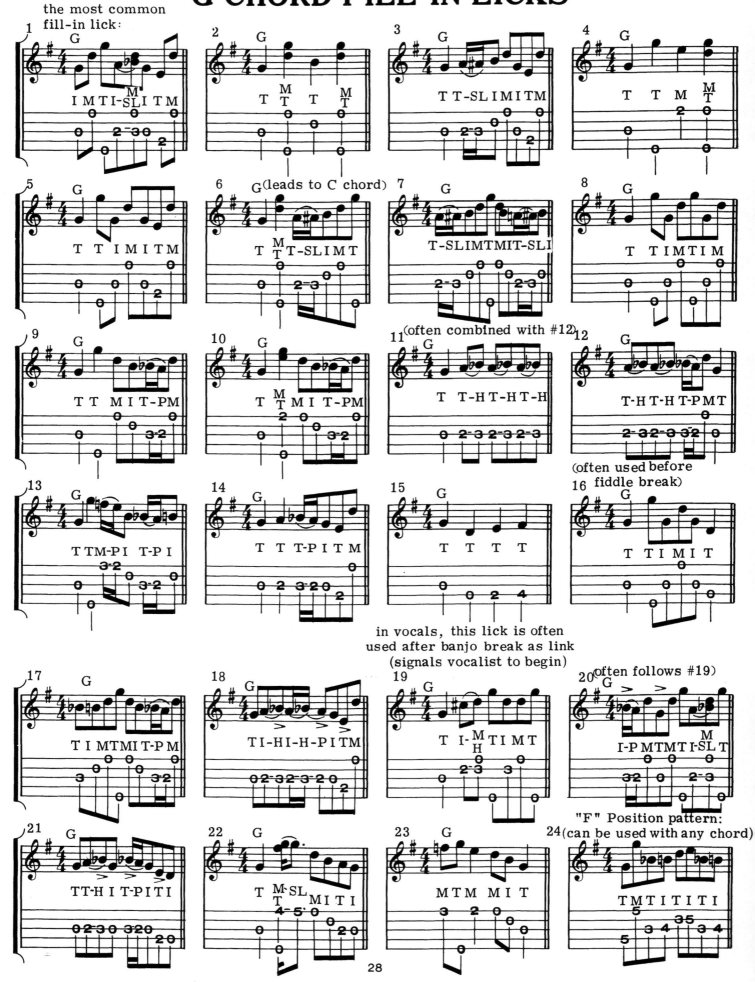

C CHORD FILL-IN LICKS

D CHORD FILL-IN LICKS

CHORD PROGRESSION
USING FILL-IN LICKS

* Note: to end the song, substitute these licks for the final two licks above:
   vocal ending:

FILL-IN LICKS
ADDITIONAL FUNCTIONS

1. Fill-In licks are often used to draw a lead break to a close. For example, they are frequently used for the D chord, just before the final G chord, (in the key of G). Also, they frequently are combined with one another to form the back-up for the B section to a melody, (as in Cripple Creek).

2. Fill-In licks are often used to lead from one chord to a different chord. In other words, they contain passing tones, which lead to the new chord. For example, for a D chord fill-in lick to lead to a G chord, (functioning as in #1 above), the following notes can be substituted in any of the D chord licks, for the last half (two beats) of the lick. These notes lead the ear to the G chord, (which should follow).

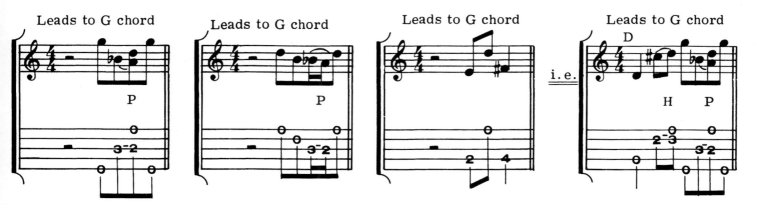

The following notes can be substituted for the last half of any of the G chord fill-in licks. The lick containing these tones will lead the ear to a C chord.

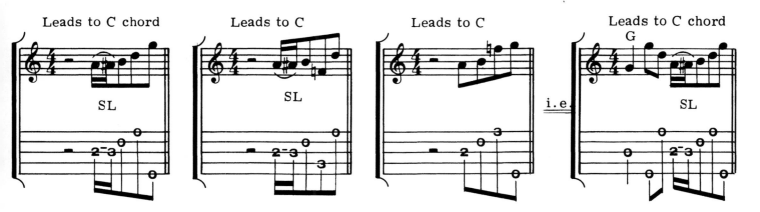

(The example for a back-up arrangement for the song,"John Hardy,"on page 41, demonstrates the use of fill-in licks containing passing tones.)

3. The examples of fill-in licks on the preceding pages are frequently combined with one another, (and with the roll patterns discussed in the following sections), according to the chords in a song, to be played as fiddle back-up. Because these licks are played on the deeper tones of the banjo, they are very effective in counter-balancing the higher tones of the fiddle. (This will be covered in more detail later on in the book.)

SONGS DEMONSTRATING
BASIC BACK-UP TECHNIQUES

The following section demonstrates how the vamping patterns, passing tones, fill-in licks and other basic back-up techniques can be used to accompany several different songs. Each song begins with a lead break containing the melody, and then gives several different back-up arrangements. The arrangements for each song are written so that you can go directly from one back-up arrangement to any other back-up arrangement, without pausing. (The "LINK" connects the different arrangements with one another.)

If you have a tape recorder, a helpful procedure for hearing the effectiveness of the various back-up arrangements is to record the lead break, and then to play the back-up arrangements along with your recording. (Remember, the back-up alone normally does not contain the melody to a song.) Pick-up notes are used to begin several of the lead breaks. These notes should only be played the first time through. If you record the lead break several times in a row without pausing, omit the pick-up notes each subsequent time. (The "link" replaces the pick-up notes after the first time.)

When playing through the back-up arrangements, think of each measure as a back-up pattern or lick. Although the last example for each song is the most advanced arrangement rhythmically, keep in mind that it is **NOT** necessarily the most effective. Often, back-up with a simple vamping rhythm, (repeating the same pattern over and over), is the best accompaniment. **When you are actually playing back-up, LISTEN** to the instrument playing the melody (lead) in order to determine which back-up patterns are most effective.

NOTE: Remember to pick the strings near the fingerboard with the right hand (in the "Y" position), when the left hand plays the chords up-the-neck (on higher fret numbers).

WABASH CANNONBALL

This tune follows essentially the same chord progression used in the exercises following each discussion. (The only difference is in how long (number of measures) you stay on each chord.)

LEAD BREAK: record this break; then play each back-up arrangement along with your recording.

Repeat the lead break without pausing, or begin playing back-up without pausing. The final measure of the lead break is the connecting <u>link</u>. (To end the song, for the last time, simply play the open 3rd string.)

WABASH CANNONBALL
BACK-UP

BACK-UP: USING THE BASIC VAMPING PATTERN: (p.17)

BACK-UP: CHANGING CHORD POSITIONS: (p.21)

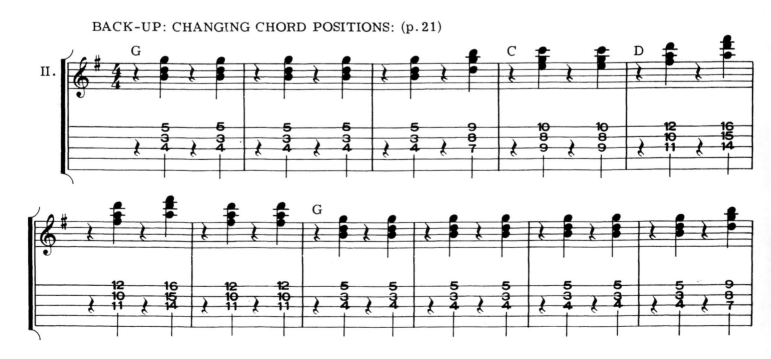

VAMPING WITH SPLIT CHORDS, USING PATTERN #2: (p.19)

COMBINING VAMPING PATTERNS--Each measure contains a vamping pattern: (pp.17-19)

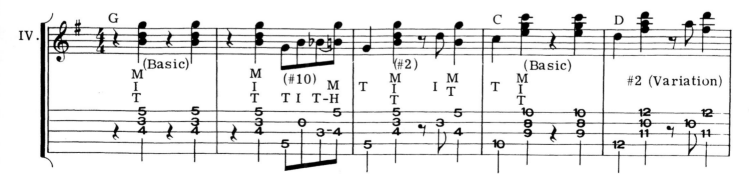

USING PASSING TONES: (to lead to new chord) (pp. 23-26)

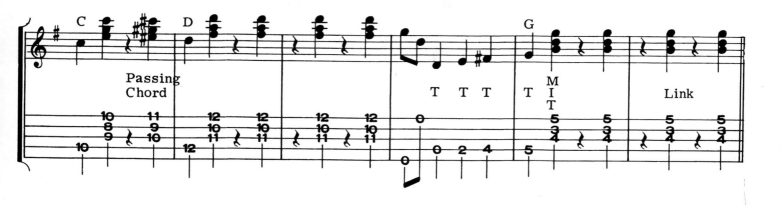

USING FILL-IN LICKS: (to fill in the pauses & as a link with the next break--back-up or lead)
(pp. 28-29)

NOTE: When you are playing back-up for a vocalist, you may have to play more than one fill-in
lick when he pauses to take a breath. (Simply play fill-in licks until he begins singing-
then return to vamping.)

COMBINING VAMPING PATTERNS & BACK-UP TECHNIQUES:

To end, play only the 1st note of the last measure (the link).
NOTE: For other back-up arrangements for this song see:

pages: 75--Scruggs-style on deep tones
101--Up-the-neck Scruggs-style
207--slow song style

JOHN HARDY

This tune uses the primary chords of the key of G, but begins on the C chord, rather than on the G chord.

LEAD:
Key of G

Repeat the lead break without pausing (do not play the pick up notes), or begin playing back-up without pausing.

JOHN HARDY
BACK-UP

BACK-UP USING THE BASIC VAMPING PATTERN: (p.17)

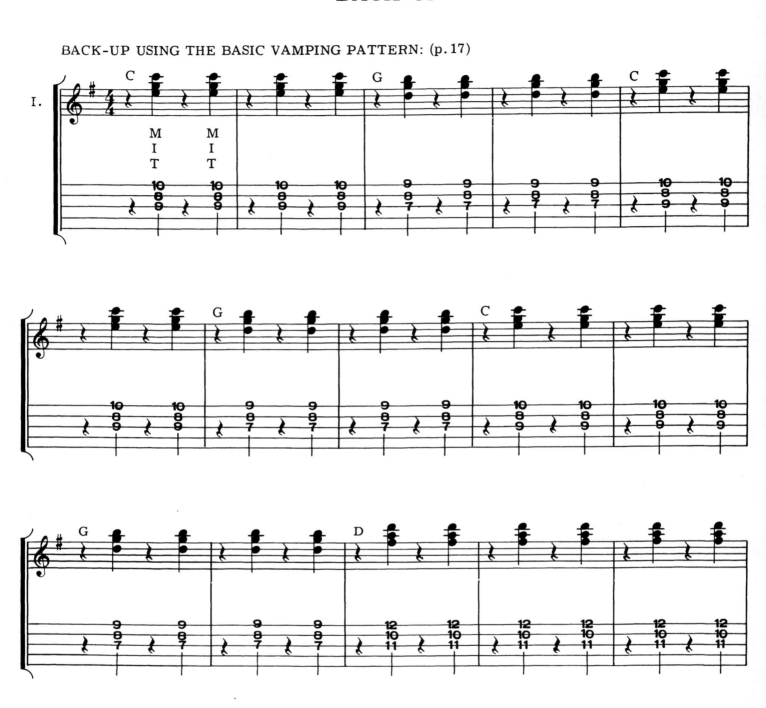

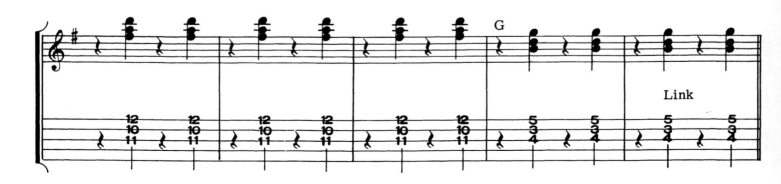

ADDING FILL-IN LICKS: (the extra long D chord allows for greater variety in the back-up)
(p.28-29)

USING PASSING TONES: (Passing chords are used to lead the music from the final D chord
to the G chord) (p.25)

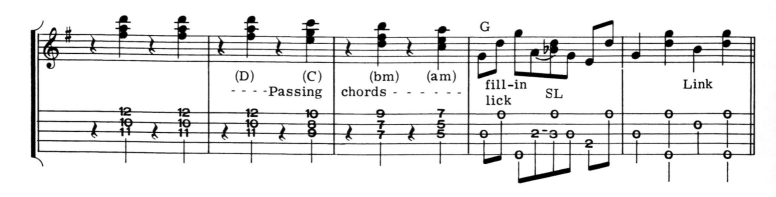

RHYTHMIC EMBELLISHMENT USING VAMPING PATTERNS #10, #2, & #12: (for practice, try playing through this chord progression using several of the other vamping patterns from p. 19)

*Note: The open 2nd string tone in pattern #10 is correct. Although it sounds dissonant when the pattern is played slowly, it is effective when used as back-up with any chord--in fact this vamping pattern is often used as the primary back-up pattern.

COMBINING BACK-UP TECHNIQUES:

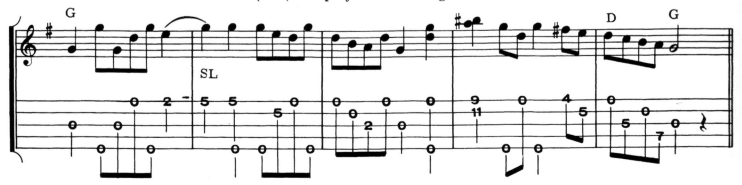

*ENDING: OMIT last measure (link) and play the following:

CRIPPLE CREEK

The chord progression for this song calls for a quick change from C to G and also from D to G at the end of each phrase. The back-up can work to make these chord changes more effective.
NOTE: play each line twice.

BACK-UP

BACK-UP--USING THE BASIC VAMPING PATTERN: p.17

CHANGING CHORD POSITIONS FOR EMBELLISHMENT:

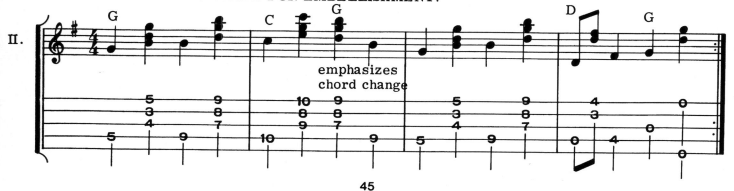

emphasizes
chord change

ADDING FILL-IN LICKS: (pp 28-29)

COMBINING BACK-UP TECHNIQUES & ADDING RHYTHMIC EMBELLISHMENT:

* Note: The 2-5 slide on the 4th string is often used to connect one break with the next.

CUMBERLAND GAP

Play through each arrangement twice. (Because the em chord is the relative minor of the G chord, the back-up can also play G for the em.)

BACK-UP

ADDING FILL-IN LICKS: pp. 28-29

COMBINING BACK-UP TECHNIQUES--plus rhythmic embellishment:

SALT RIVER

Salt River is a traditional fiddle tune which is played as an instrumental. For this reason, the vamping style of back-up is very effective for this song.

BACK-UP

BACK-UP USING THE BASIC VAMPING PATTERN: (p.17)

EMBELLISHMENT--Adding passing tones & fill-in licks and changing from one position of a chord to another position: (Notice that the fill-in licks drive the back-up to the end of the phrases.)

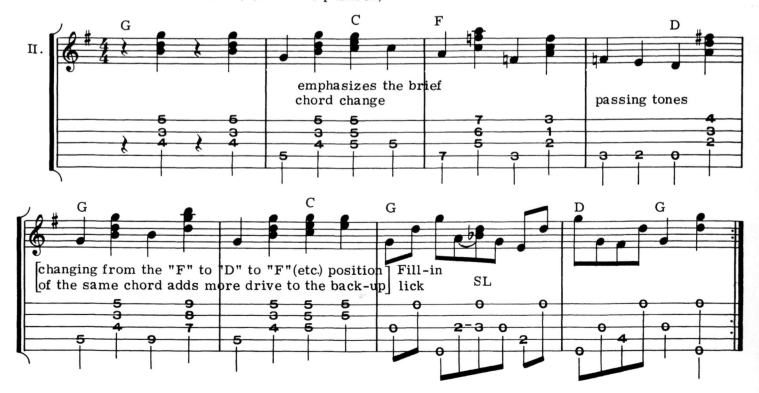

RHYTHMIC EMBELLISHMENT--"Splitting chords": In addition to the vamping patterns on p. 19, the following back-up arrangement contains additional patterns. (The possibilities for rhythmic variety are virtually infinite.)

COMBINING BACK-UP TECHNIQUES: think of each measure as a vamping pattern, fill-in lick, etc.

SCRUGGS-STYLE BACK-UP

The following section of this book will be concerned with a fairly active style of back-up which is frequently referred to as "Scruggs-Style" back-up. In addition to Earl Scruggs, who helped to develop and popularize this style of back-up, many other banjo players, (including Snuffy Jenkins, Ralph Stanley, Don Reno, J.D. Crowe, and Alan Munde) have also contributed to the development of this style of back-up as it is played today.

Scruggs-style back-up can be used to accompany songs played by any instrument, at any tempo, and it is especially effective as back-up for singing and for the fiddle. ("Vamping" is often the preferred style of back-up for the guitar and the dobro; the timbre (tone quality) of the banjo is very similar to the timbre of those instruments, and it may tend to compete with them if it is very active during their lead breaks. However, Scruggs-style back-up can, at times, be very effective behind these instruments, also.)

Scruggs-style back-up consists primarily of combinations of specific right hand fingering patterns which are played while holding chord positions for the chords in a song with the left hand. The same fingering patterns can be used to form the back-up for many different songs. These patterns are the blocks with which the back-up arrangements are built, (according to the chords of the songs).

There are basically three types of back-up patterns used in Scruggs-Style back-up:

1. The Standard Roll Patterns--which provide the basic foundation for this style of back-up;

2. Lick Patterns--which can be played while holding any chord with the left hand;

3 Licks--which can be played only for specific chords.

The following section will discuss these back-up patterns according to the area of the fingerboard in which the back-up is played. An introduction to the Standard Roll Patterns, which provide the basis for this style of back-up, will begin the section. This will be followed by a detailed discussion of Scruggs-style back-up as it is played using the deep tones of the banjo, (near the peghead in the 1st-5th fret area of the fingerboard). Following the songs demonstrating back-up played in this area of the fingerboard, is a detailed discussion of Scruggs-Style back-up as it is played up-the-neck, with the higher pitched tones of the banjo, along with songs demonstrating back-up played in this area of the fingerboard.

THE STANDARD ROLL PATTERNS

The Standard Roll Patterns provide the basic foundation for Scruggs-style back-up. Each roll pattern is a <u>right hand</u> fingering pattern, consisting of eight (eighth) notes, which can be played while holding <u>any</u> chord position with the left hand. (One pattern is equal to one measure of music or tablature.) When used as back-up, the same pattern can be repeated over and over throughout an entire song, (while the left hand changes chords as required), or the roll patterns can be combined with one another and with the variations and back-up licks discussed in the following pages. The roll patterns can also be used to embellish the vamping style of back-up, especially when the chords are played high on the fingerboard, near the head of the banjo. These roll patterns can be used as back-up for any song played at any tempo.

EACH PATTERN CAN BE PLAYED WHILE HOLDING ANY CHORD WITH THE LEFT HAND!

FORWARD ROLL: TIMTIMTI

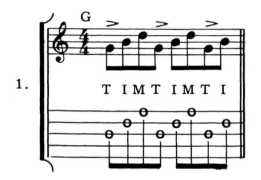

1.

BACKWARD ROLL: MITMITMI

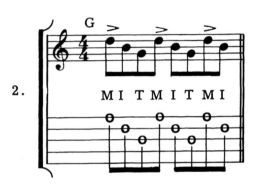

2.

MIXED ROLL: TITMTITM

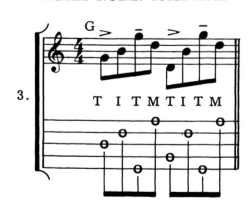

3.

FORWARD-REVERSE: TIMTMITM

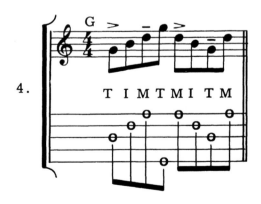

4.

NOTE: when a song uses two chords in the same measure, divide the roll pattern between the chords. (i.e. Play the first four notes of the roll pattern for one chord, and the second four notes for the other chord.)

The following chord progressions can be used as back-up for the songs listed on page 18. Notice that each measure, (between the bar lines), consists of one of the standard right hand roll patterns.

CHORD PROGRESSION
(USING THE FORWARD ROLL)

The Forward Roll Pattern is used for each measure in the following chord progression.

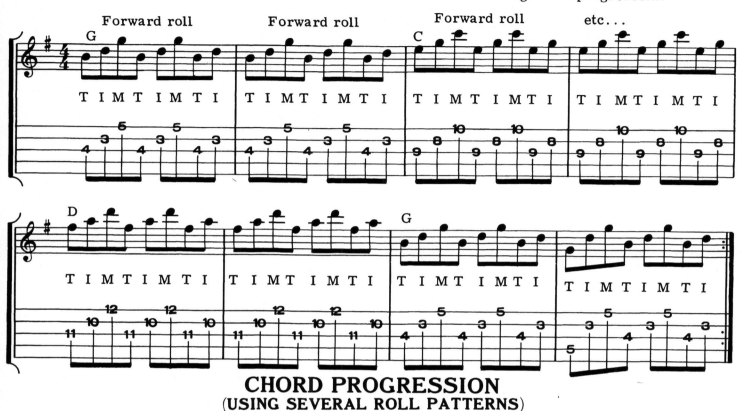

CHORD PROGRESSION
(USING SEVERAL ROLL PATTERNS)

Each measure in the following progression uses a different standard roll pattern.

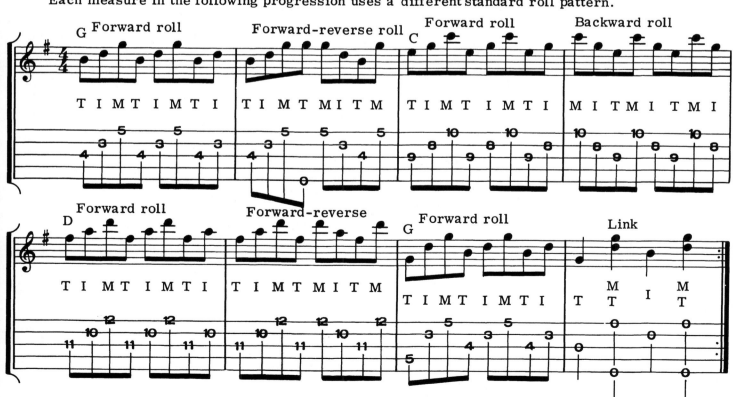

55

SCRUGGS-STYLE BACK-UP
USING THE DEEP TONES OF THE BANJO
OPEN-5TH FRETS

Scruggs-style back-up is effective for any instrumental or vocal lead break when it is played with the deeper tones of the banjo, (holding chord positions near the peghead of the banjo--from the 1st-5th frets). However, it is particularly effective when it is used to accompany fiddle, mandolin, and vocal lead breaks. The deeper tones of the banjo counter-balance the higher pitched tones of the fiddle and mandolin, and the activity of the roll patterns creates a counter-melody which enhances the effectiveness of the melody. The back-up for a vocalist frequently <u>begins</u> with the deeper tones of the banjo. The back-up can remain in this area of the finger-board throughout the song, or it can move up-the-neck as the song progresses, increasing the intensity of the back-up. (Keep in mind that these are only suggestions which are based upon common practice...anything is possible   The key to effective back-up is to LISTEN to what you are playing in relation to what the lead instrument and the other back-up instruments are playing.)

The Standard Roll Patterns can be used effectively as back-up for any chord played in the deeper tonal area of the fingerboard. These patterns can be played in their basic form, or they can be varied. Slides and other left hand techniques can be added to the basic form of the roll patterns, for example. Also, the rhythm of the roll pattern can be varied by substituting a quarter note for two eighth notes (♩ for ♫), for example, or by syncopating the rhythm of the roll pattern. Also, each roll pattern can begin with any finger on any string. Remember, <u>the name of the roll pattern is determined by the order in which the fingers pick the strings</u>, not by which finger begins the roll pattern. (The Forward Roll played on the deeper tones of the banjo frequently begins with the Index finger rather than with the thumb. However, the roll still has 8 ♪ notes.)

The following chord progressions demonstrate how back-up can be played using the Standard Roll patterns on the deeper tones of the banjo for the songs listed on page 18. Included in these are examples of some of the common ways these patterns can be varied. Keep in mind when playing through these chord progressions that <u>each measure of music consists of a roll pattern</u>.

Following the chord progressions will be discussions concerning the various ways to embellish the back-up played in this area of the fingerboard, and finally songs, to demonstrate how back-up can be played on the deeper tones of the banjo.

1. THE FORWARD ROLL:  (basic right hand pattern)

This pattern is responsible for much of the rhythmic drive evident in a tune when it is played by a bluegrass band. (The drive is even visible in the slant of the tablature: ///).

CHORD PROGRESSION
using the Forward Roll with chords held in the open-5th fret area of the fingerboard

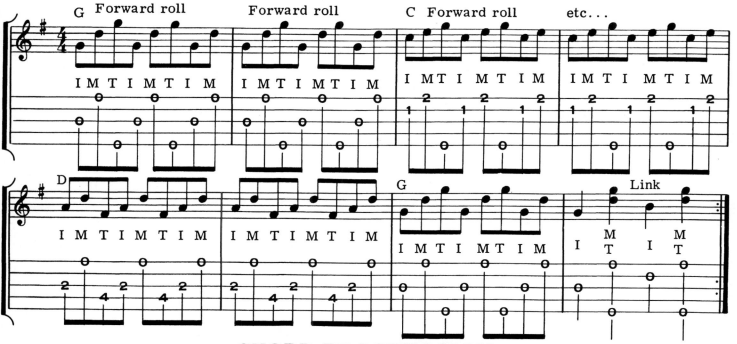

CHORD PROGRESSION
using the Forward Roll and its variations

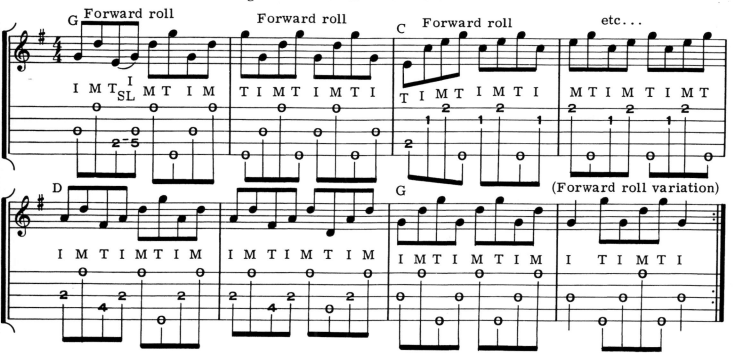

NOTE: Two forward roll patterns can be combined by simply playing the same right hand fingering twice, (as the 1st two measures of the 1st chord progression above demonstrate); or the right fingers can continue rolling for two measures (16 eighth notes) in the same direction, (as in the 1st two measures of the 2nd chord progression).

NOTE: Avoid picking the open 2nd string if possible with the open G chord, for it tends to add too much color, and may compete with the lead.

2. THE BACKWARD ROLL: 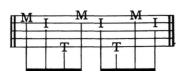 (basic right hand pattern)

Notice when playing through this pattern, that the right hand fingers are "rolling" in the opposite direction from that of the Forward Roll Pattern. The Backward Roll Pattern is usually used in combination with other roll patterns when the back-up is played with the deeper tones of the banjo, rather than serving as the primary back-up pattern throughout the song. As is true of all of the Standard Roll patterns, the Backward Roll can be used while holding any chord with the left hand, and the right thumb can pick the 3rd, 4th, or 5th string. For example:

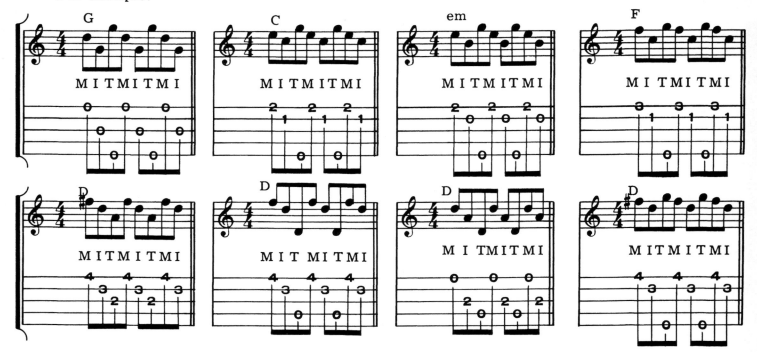

CHORD PROGRESSION
combining the Backward Roll and the Forward Roll Patterns

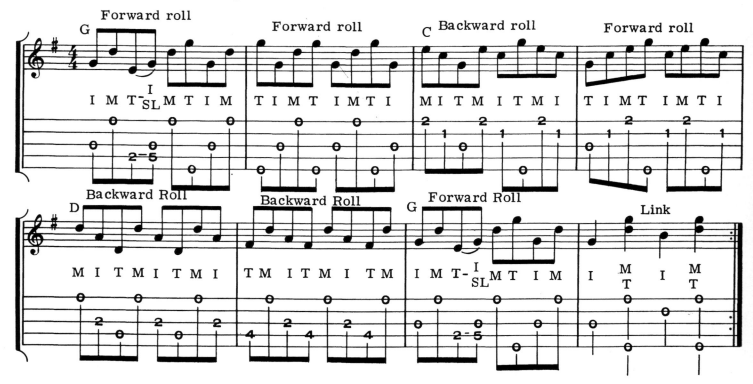

58

3. THE MIXED ROLL:  (the thumb picks every other note)

CHORD PROGRESSION
using the Mixed Roll Pattern

Although this pattern can be used with songs played at any tempo, it is a popular back-up pattern for songs which are sung or played at a fairly slow tempo, when the back-up is played on the deep tones of the banjo.

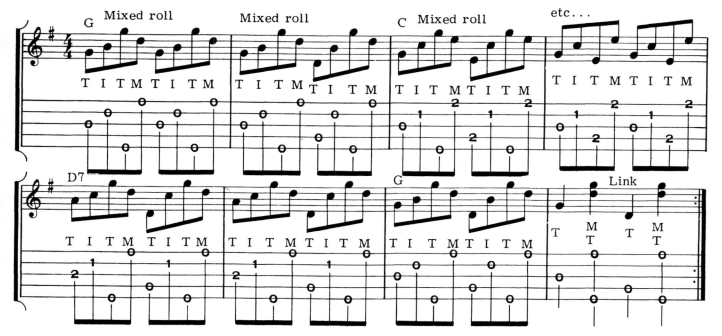

CHORD PROGRESSION
using Mixed Roll Variations

This progression exemplifies a fairly typical Scruggs-style back-up arrangement, played with chords in the open-5th fret area of the banjo. It can be used as back-up for songs played at any tempo. The pattern used for the C and D chords is a very common back-up pattern for these chords when they are played in the first position, (between the nut and the 5th fret). (Notice that an extra tone is added to these chords which adds color and also acts as a passing tone within the roll pattern.)

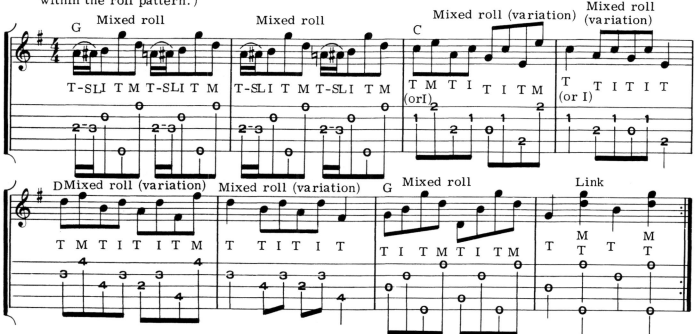

NOTE: For practice, substitute a G chord Forward Roll pattern for each measure containing a G chord in the above progression.

4. THE FORWARD-REVERSE ROLL:

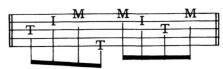

This roll pattern is a very popular back-up pattern for playing on the deeper tones of the banjo, and it is frequently used as the primary back-up pattern throughout a song. As is true with each of the standard rolls, this right hand fingering pattern can be used while holding ANY chord with the left hand. i.e.:

Also, the right thumb can pick either the 3rd, 4th or 5th string:

CHORD PROGRESSION
using the Forward-Reverse Roll

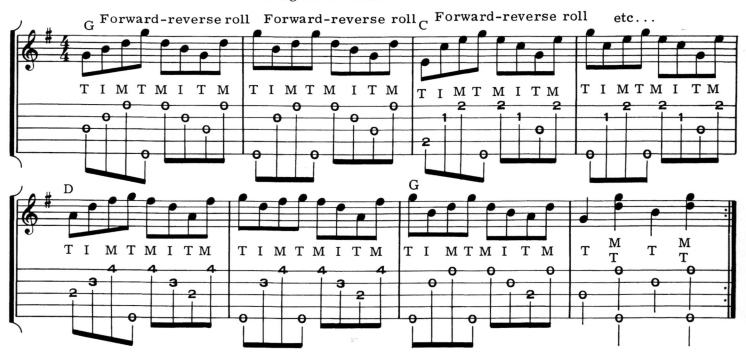

NOTE: When combining two of these roll patterns, the same pattern can be played twice in a row. However, frequently, the 5th string begins the second pattern, (as in measures #2, #4 and #6 in the above progression.)

VARIATIONS OF THE FORWARD-REVERSE ROLL PATTERN

 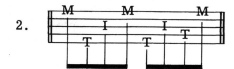

Although these patterns are not generally used as the primary roll patterns throughout an entire back-up arrangement, they are <u>frequently</u> used along with the other roll patterns. These patterns can be used while holding ANY chord with the left hand.

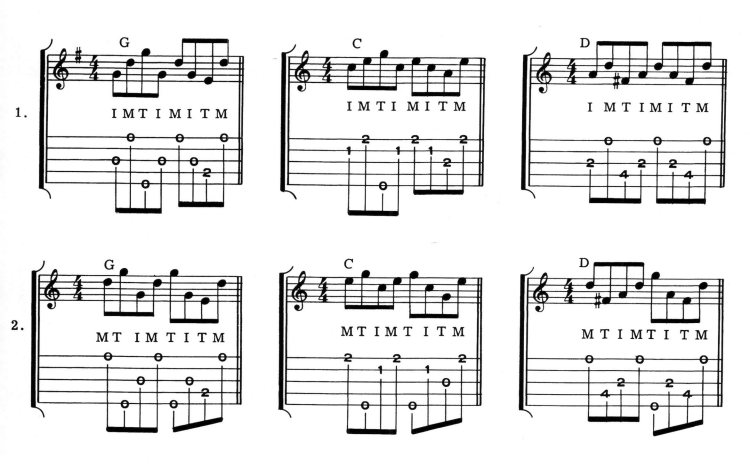

As is true with any back-up pattern, the rhythm of these variations can also be altered:

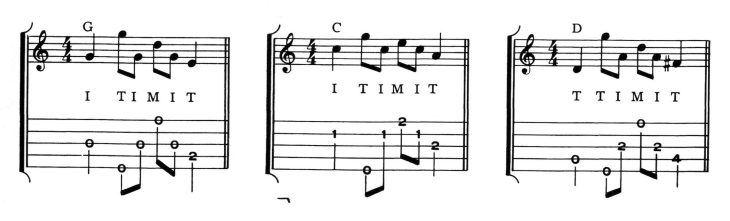

61

COMMONLY USED G, C, & D CHORD PATTERNS

Because the G, C, and D chords employ open strings when they are played with the deeper tones of the banjo, and because these chords are used so frequently in back-up played on the banjo, several variations of the standard roll patterns have become widely used in back-up when playing each of these chords. The examples below are listed according to the chord for which they are used.

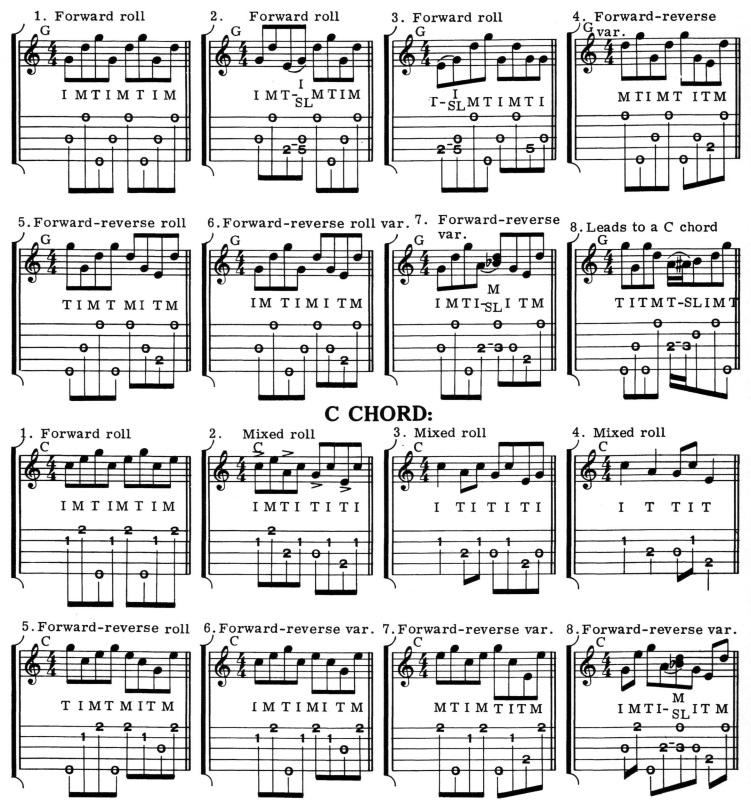

D CHORD:

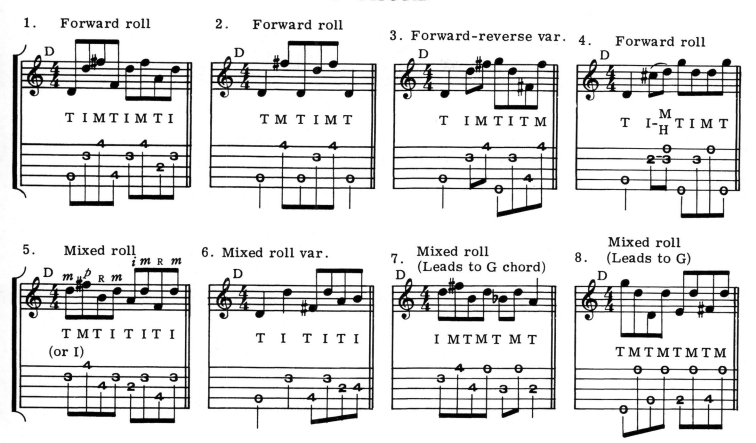

NOTE: Variations of above patterns #5, #6, #7, and #8 can also be played with open strings as follows:

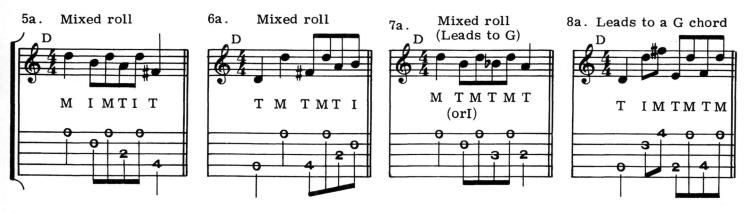

NOTE: the above roll pattern variations are useful particularly in the Keys of G, C and D, which are frequently used keys for back-up on the banjo. Notice that each key uses these chords:
KEY of G: primary chords are G, C, & D.
KEY of C: primary chords are C, F, & G.
KEY of D: primary chords are D, G, & A.

Each measure in the following chord progressions contains a standard roll pattern.

CHORD PROGRESSION
combining standard roll patterns

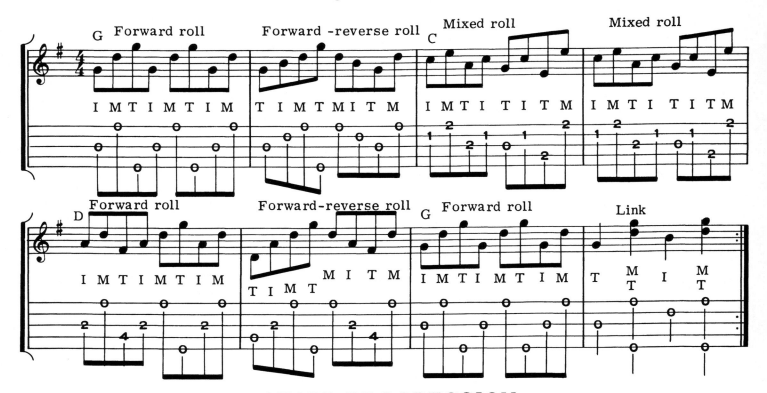

CHORD PROGRESSION
combining standard roll pattern variations

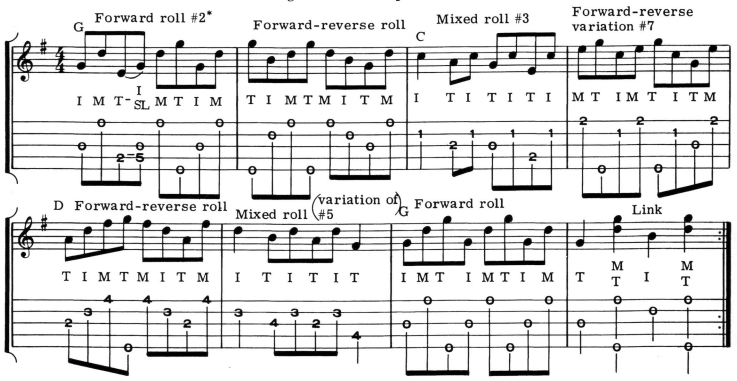

*Note: the # above the measures correspond to the examples on p 62 of patterns for G, C, or D chords.

PASSING TONES

Non-harmonic tones, such as "Passing Tones", (described on p.23), can contribute greatly
to the overall effectiveness of Scruggs-style back-up. The following examples are frequently
used to lead the ear of the listener from one chord to another chord, when the back-up is played on the deeper tones of the banjo. The "passing tones" are played for the chord indicated,
just before the change to the new chord.

G CHORD PASSING TONES:

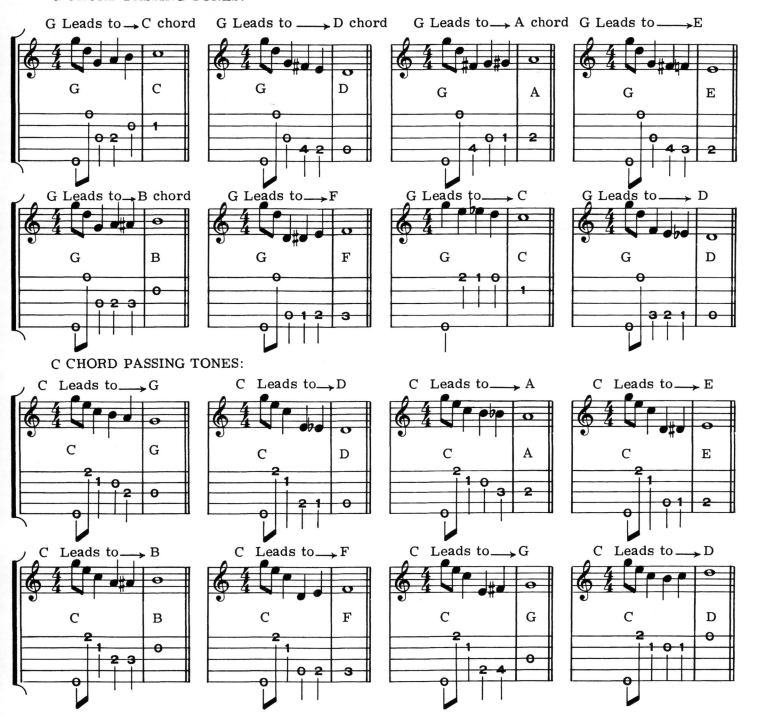

C CHORD PASSING TONES:

NOTE: Only for those interested in music theory:
(Neighboring tones, cambiata, and escape tones are correct theoretical terms for several of
the non-harmonic tones in the above examples. However, the function for each of these is the
same--to lead the music from one chord to another chord.)

D CHORD PASSING TONES:

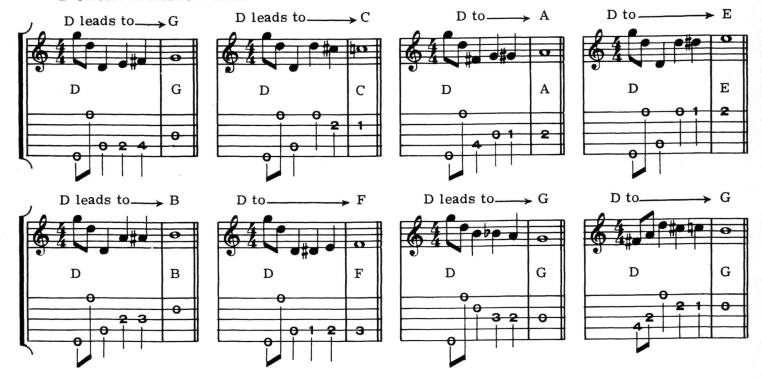

CHORD PROGRESSION
using roll patterns and passing tones

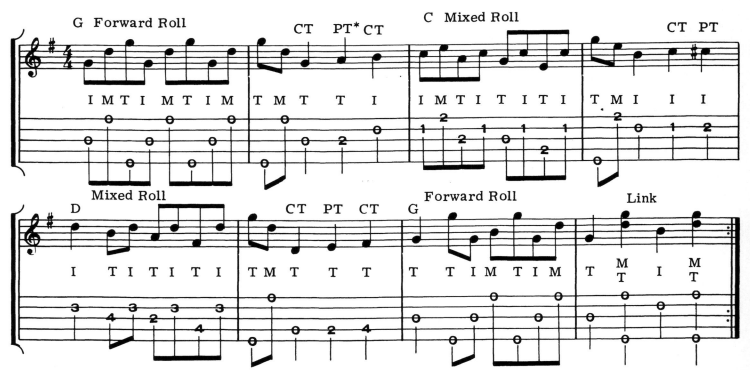

*PT means Passing Tones (see p. 23 for definition)
CT means Chord Tone

ROLL PATTERNS USING PASSING TONES

Passing tones can also be incorporated into the roll patterns, resulting in "licks" which are used only for specific chords. The following "licks" are formed from the Mixed Roll pattern, and are frequently used to embellish the back-up while it stays on the same chord for two measures. Each of the following examples can be followed by ANY chord; the passing tones are not used to change chords, but instead are used only to embellish the chord for which they are played.

NOTE: These patterns are especially effective for fiddle back-up.

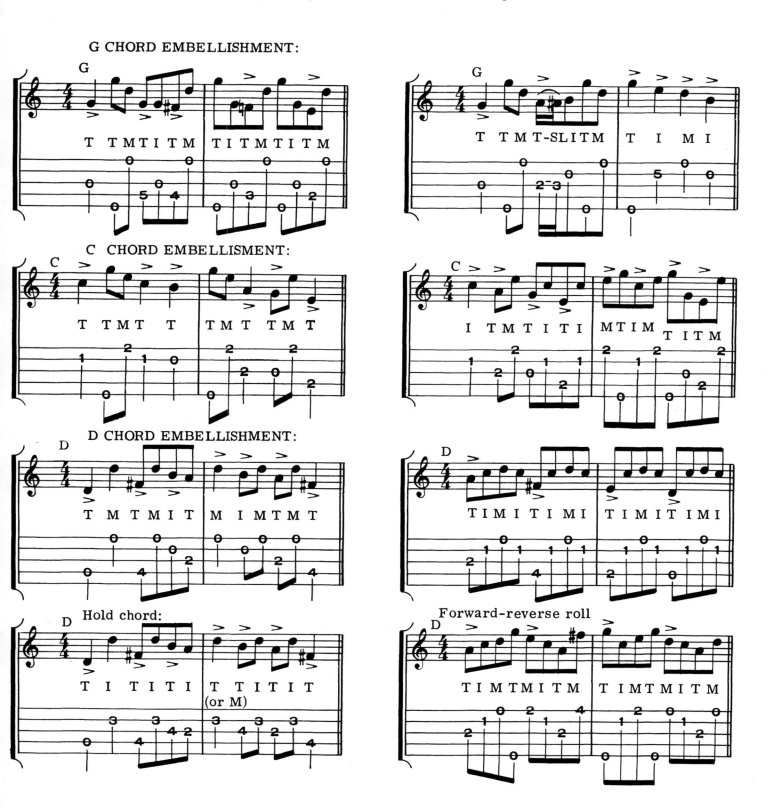

The examples of roll patterns containing passing tones on the preceding page can be used to embellish the back-up, as occurs with the C chord in the first chord progression below, or they can be used as primary back-up patterns as in the second chord progression, which uses a roll pattern with passing tones for each chord in the progression.

CHORD PROGRESSION
rolls, passing tones, licks
(embellishment)

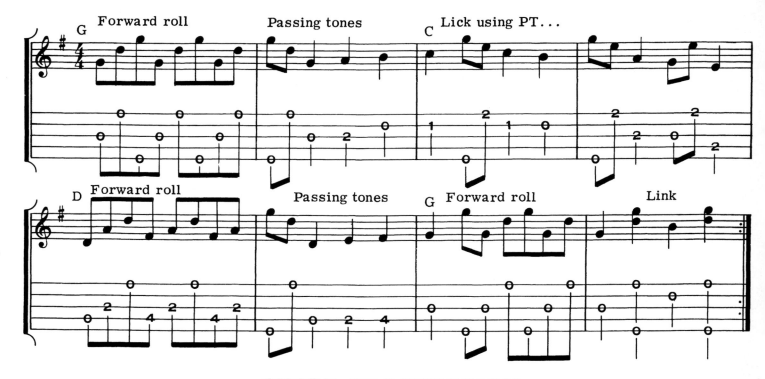

CHORD PROGRESSION
combining roll patterns containing passing tones
(as primary back-up patterns)

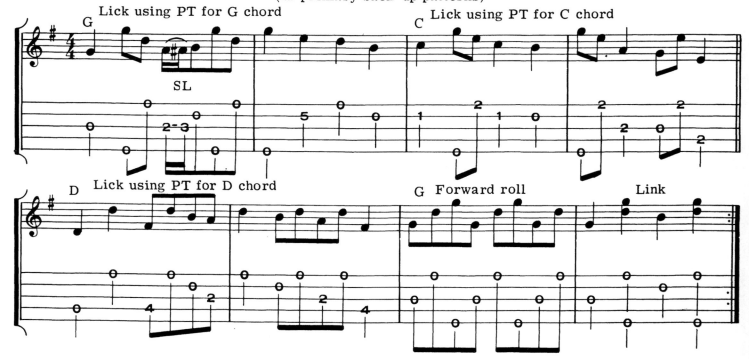

LICKS USING PASSING TONES

Due to the nature of music* certain chords are frequently followed by other specific chords. For example, in many songs, G often leads to C; D often leads to G; and A often leads to D. As a result, certain licks have evolved which have the same function as that of playing passing tones, (to lead the music from one specific chord to another specific chord). Each of the following licks is commonly used in Scruggs-style back-up for the chords indicated. (Each lick contains passing tones which lead to the new chord.) See p.31 also.

G CHORD LICKS WHICH LEAD TO C: (The following licks should be played just before a C chord)

D CHORD LICKS WHICH LEAD TO G: (The following licks should be followed with a G chord pattern.)

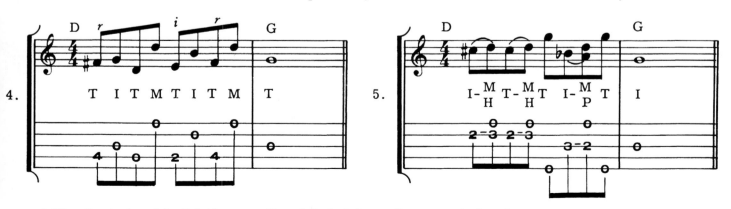

* The first chord is 5 letters up the alphabet from the second chord, which results in a V-I progression. In music, the V chord is frequently followed by its I chord.

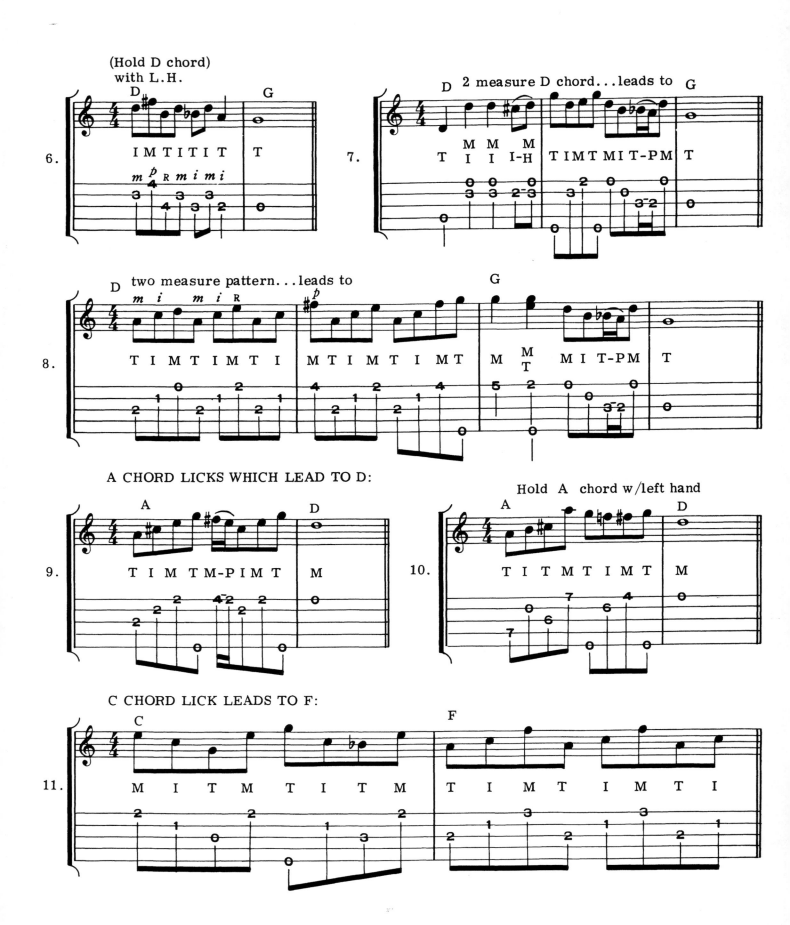

CHORD PROGRESSION

using licks to lead to new chords

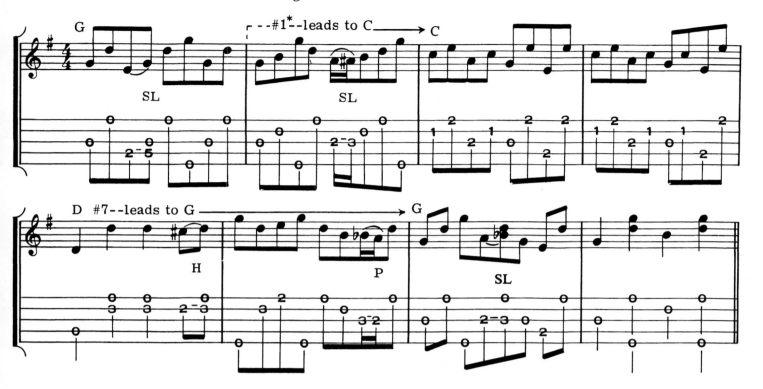

CHORD PROGRESSION

using licks to change chords

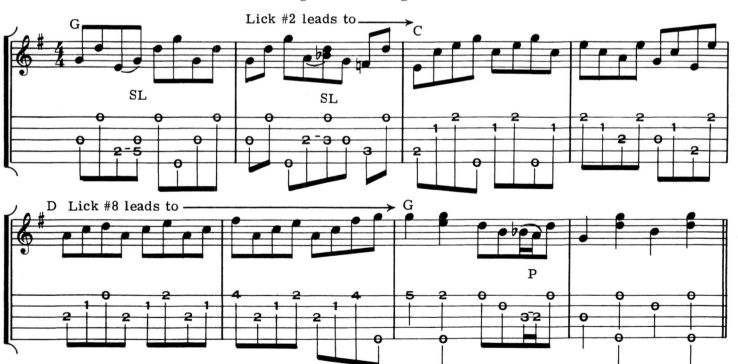

*NOTE: The number above the licks which contain passing tones corresponds to one of the licks on pp.69-70.

FILL-IN LICKS

Fill-in licks are used in Scruggs-style back-up in the same manner described on p.27, (i.e. to fill in the pauses in the melody line--as punctuation, to draw the back-up to a close, etc.) In addition to these functions, Scruggs-style back-up often combines these licks according to the chords of the song, (in the same manner that the roll patterns are combined), when the back-up is played on the deeper tones of the banjo. Generally the faster the song is played, the greater the number of fill-in licks used. (A back-up arrangement can consist only of fill-in licks, or these licks can be combined with the standard roll patterns and passing tones.) The following chord progressions demonstrate the uses of fill-in licks in Scruggs-style back-up. The number above each fill-in lick corresponds to the same lick on pp.28&29. Refer to those pages for additional examples of fill-in licks, and for additional information concerning their function in back-up.

CHORD PROGRESSION
using fill-in licks to punctuate the back-up

CHORD PROGRESSION
using fill-in licks as primary back-up licks

RHYTHMIC EMBELLISHMENT

Another very effective method for embellishing the back-up to enhance the effectiveness of a song, is that of altering the rhythm of the roll patterns or the licks, to fit the overall rhythmic nature of the song. In this manner, for example, "drive", or "bounce" can be added to a song, or a certain area of a song might be emphasized through syncopation of the rhythm in that part of the song. When working with rhythm, it is important to remember that the basic pulse of a song (i.e. the beats per measure), remains the same; where the notes are placed (played) within the context of that pulse determines the effect the rhythm has on the song. The following are frequently used methods of rhythmic embellishment:

1. Fill in the pauses created by quarter notes (♩) by playing two eighth notes (♫) for each quarter note in a lick or roll. This adds <u>drive</u> or forward motion to a song.

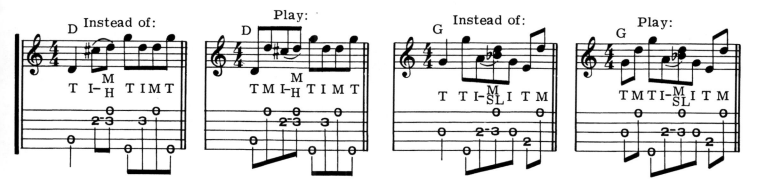

2. Picking the same string twice in a row can add bounce to a song. The first example below picks the same tone twice in a row; the second example replaces the pull-off with single string picking. (Picking a string twice, rather than using a pull-off, hammer, slide, etc. is an effective method for adding bounce to a slower song. J.D. Crowe frequently uses this technique in his back-up.)

Instead of:

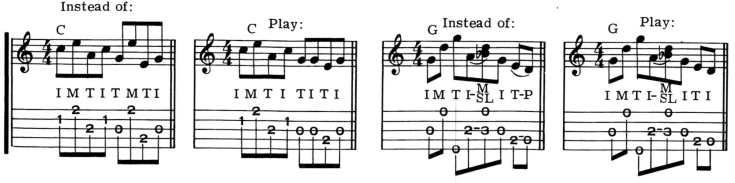

3. Syncopation of the basic rhythm is a common practice in back-up. When the rhythm is syncopated, the accent is placed on a weak beat instead of a strong beat. For example, generally, the accent is the strongest on the first beat of a measure. If the first note of a roll pattern or lick is replaced with a rest, the accent will then fall on the second note, which is usually unaccented. This results in syncopation of the rhythm. i.e.:

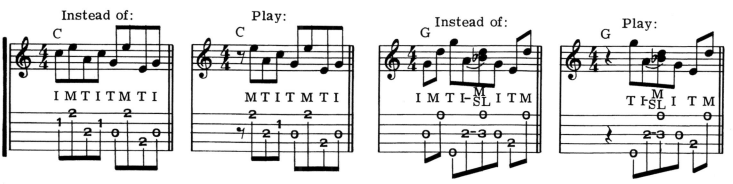

SONGS
SCRUGGS-STYLE BACK-UP
OPEN-5TH FRETS

The following back-up arrangements demonstrate how the same rolls & licks can be used to form the back-up played on the deeper tones of the banjo for several different songs. When playing through these songs, don't be frustrated by the similarity of the arrangements. That is the point of this entire book!--to provide you with patterns that can be used as back-up for many different songs. Back-up is normally NOT concerned with playing a melody. Its primary concern is harmonic and rhythmic--working with chords and rhythm to provide support for the lead instrument. Play through the lead break for each song on a tape recorder, if possible. Once you have recorded the lead, play the back-up along with the melody. Although the back-up arrangements are quite similar when compared with one another, each song should sound completely different from the other when the back-up is played along with the melody of the song. (If the lead break does not appear with the back-up arrangement for a song, refer to the page number in the book where the lead break does appear. Several of the same songs are used throughout this book,to demonstrate how different back-up techniques and styles can be used for the same songs. The lead break, however, only appears once for each song.)

REVIEW

Before playing through the back-up arrangements, it may be helpful to review the major points concerned with back-up played on the deeper tones of the banjo, (1st-5th fret area)(pp. 56-73)

1. The Standard Roll Patterns are the basic foundation of Scruggs-style back-up--it is IMPORTANT to KNOW these.(p. 54) Each roll pattern is a right hand fingering pattern that can be used as back-up while holding ANY chord with the left hand.(pp. 57-61)
2. Back-up played in this area of the fingerboard is frequently used to accompany the fiddle, the mandolin, or a vocalist.
3. Certain variations of the roll patterns are commonly used for the G, C, and D chords when the back-up is played with the deeper tones of the banjo.(see pp. 62-63)
4. Polish can be added to the back-up through the use of:

    a. Passing tones: to lead the music from one chord tone to another(pp. 65-71)
    b. Fill-in licks: as punctuation(p. 72)
       as links to connect one verse or break with the next
       as primary back-up licks for fast songs
    c. Rhythmic embellishment(p. 73)

WABASH CANNONBALL
BACK-UP

A lead break for this tune can be found on p. 33. Each measure in the following arrangement (back-up) contains a back-up lick or roll pattern. (The no. (#) with each lick corresponds to its example on page 62.) For practice substitute other licks for these chords.

BACK-UP:

To end the back-up, play only the first note of the "link". Play the entire link to connect this arrangement with the lead break or with another back-up arr.

Note: Other back-up arrangements for this tune can be found on the following pages: 34-38, 101-106, 207-208.

JOHN HARDY
BACK-UP

A lead break for this tune can be found on p. 39. Notice when playing through the following arrangement, that each measure contains a roll pattern or a lick, which is played for the applicable chord in the chord progression of the song. This arrangement would be effective as back-up for a fiddle or mandolin lead break, and it would also be effective as back-up when someone is singing the song.

BACK-UP:

NOTE: Other back-up arrangements for this tune can be found on pages: 40-44, 107-111.

EAST VIRGINIA
LEAD

This song is normally performed as a singing song, and can be played either fast or slow.
(Remember, the back-up begins with the first full measure, not with the pick-up notes.)

LEAD:

To back-up (or repeat lead omitting pick-up notes).

EAST VIRGINIA
BACK-UP

The following back-up arrangement is very typical of Scruggs-style back-up played with the deeper tones of the banjo. This particular arrangement can also be used as back-up for the songs: "Lonesome Road Blues", "Going Down That Road Feeling Bad", and "There's More Pretty Girls Than One", for they use exactly the same chord progression.

BACK-UP:

NOTE: Other back-up arrangements for this song can be found on pages: 119

NEW RIVER TRAIN
LEAD

The following arrangement is a lead break which can be played on the banjo for the song, "New River Train". This song is generally played at a fairly rapid tempo. (A back-up arrangement is on the following page, and also on pages 112, 113 and 114.)

LEAD BREAK:

ALSO--try playing the back-up for "Red River Valley" (pp. 129-134), along with the above lead break. ("New River Train" and "Red River Valley use the same chord progression!)

NEW RIVER TRAIN
BACK-UP

The songs, "New River Train", "Roll In My Sweet Baby's Arms", "Red River Valley", "Mama Don't Allow", "May I Sleep In Your Barn Tonight, Mister?", "Why Don't You Tell Me So?", "Will You Be Lovin' Another Man?", and "When The Saints Go Marchin' In", use the same chord progression. Therefore, the following back-up arrangement can be used for any of these songs when they are played in the Key of G. (The frequent use of left hand techniques, (i.e. slides, hammers, etc.) adds drive to the back-up when the song is played at a fairly fast tempo.)

BACK-UP--Roll Patterns with the Deep Tones of the Banjo:
(effective as vocal, fiddle, or mandolin back-up)

80

LONG JOURNEY HOME
LEAD

This song is usually performed as a singing song, and it is often played at a fairly rapid tempo.

LEAD BREAK:
(Fast tempo)

Back-up arrangements for this tune can be found on pages: 82, 118 to back up...

LONG JOURNEY HOME
BACK-UP

Often, in singing songs, the vocalist may pause an extra one or two measures between verses. When this occurs, simply play fill-in licks for the same chord until he (or she) begins singing. (You may repeat the same lick, or play a different one.) See *extra link at the end of this back-up arrangement. The following arrangement uses several fill-in licks as basic back-up licks due to the tempo (fast) at which the song is played.

BACK-UP:

82

WRECK OF THE OLD 97
LEAD

This song is usually played at a rapid tempo. It is generally performed as a vocal song, often with the capo on the 5th or 7th fret, (keys of C, D).

LEAD:

To back-up (or repeat lead without pick-up notes)

WRECK OF THE OLD 97
BACK-UP

This tune uses a chord progression which is common to many bluegrass songs. The following back-up arrangement can be used to accompany any of the following tunes: "Your Love Is like A Flower", "If I Should Wander Back Tonight", "Hard Ain't It Hard", "I'm Waiting To Hear You Call Me Darling", and "Bury Me Beneath The Willow".
NOTE: for practice, try playing all* of the back-up arrangements for this tune along with the lead for "Bury Me Beneath The Willow" (p. 143).

*NOTE: Other back-up arrangements for this song can be found on pages: 115-117.

SCRUGGS-STYLE
UP-THE-NECK BACK-UP
5TH-22ND FRET

Scruggs-style back-up can be played up-the-neck (i.e. 5th-22nd frets)for any type of lead break, vocal or instrumental, played at any tempo. However, it is extremely effective when it is used to accompany a vocalist singing a song at a medium or fairly fast tempo. Generally, the back-up for a singing song will begin on the deeper tones of the banjo, and as the song progresses, the back-up will move into the higher pitched areas of the finger- board. This helps to increase the overall intensity of the song. The back-up can then remain in the up-the-neck area, it can re- turn to the lower tonal area, or it can include the entire finger- board when the vocalist is singing. (In a singing song, when an instrument takes a break, the banjo will normally play the style of back-up most appropriate for that instrument--i.e. for the fiddle, the back-up may use the Scruggs-style rolls and licks on the deeper tones of the banjo; when the vocalist again begins sing- ing, the back-up may be played up-the-neck, or in whatever manner best enhances the effectiveness of the singer.) Back-up is also often played up-the-neck when the banjo is accompanying the fiddle or mandolin in an instrumental song, (a song without singing). In this manner, the banjo is often able to create a counter- melody in the same tonal range the lead instrument is using. How- ever, the banjo normally does not remain in this area of the finger- board throughout an entire song.

The following section on up-the-neck back-up will first discuss the Standard Roll Patterns as they are played in this area of the finger- board. It will then discuss the "Licks" which are used to embellish the back-up. All of the techniques used with the vamping style of back-up, such as passing tones and fill-in licks, are also used with Scruggs-style back-up when it is played up-the-neck. (Refer to pp. 21-31 under BASIC BACK-UP Techniques for discussions of these techniques.)

Most of the patterns covered in the following section will involve holding full (all four strings) chord positions with the left hand. It is also helpful to keep in mind that the open 5th string is gener- ally avoided in up-the-neck back-up. Throughout the entire sec- tion, the roll patterns and licks should be played with the right hand positioned close to, or even over the fingerboard--well away from the bridge. (The right hand should be playing in the "Y" Position, (see p.7). This will greatly enhance the effectiveness of the banjo when it is playing back-up with the higher pitched tones of the banjo.

THE STANDARD ROLL PATTERNS

The Standard Roll Patterns discussed on p.54 provide the basis for Scruggs-style up-the-neck back-up. An effective back-up arrangement can be played using ONLY the roll patterns. The same pattern can be used over and over for each chord, or different patterns can be combined. These right hand patterns can also be combined with other back-up licks played either in the 1st-5th fret area, (such as the fill-in licks and deeper tone back-up patterns), or up-the-neck, (such as the licks discussed in the following pages under Embellishment Patterns).

NOTE: When playing through these patterns, the <u>right hand</u> should be positioned close to the fingerboard...NOT by the bridge.
NOTE: The <u>left hand</u> should hold full chord positions,(all 4 strings).
NOTE: Each roll pattern is a right hand pattern which can be played while holding ANY chord with the left hand.
NOTE: The open 5th string is generally avoided in up-the-neck back-up. The right thumb picks either the 3rd or 4th string, unless the 5th string is fretted.

1. <u>THE</u> <u>FORWARD</u> <u>ROLL</u>:

This pattern is often used as the primary back-up pattern for a song. (The following examples can be played as a chord progression.)
NOTE: The right thumb can pick either the 3rd or 4th string.
NOTE: Hold the chord indicated with the left hand.

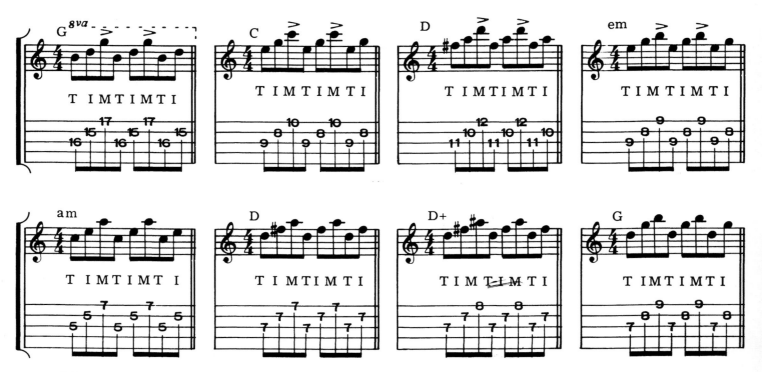

(The accent generally falls on the 1st string, when this pattern is played up-the-neck.)

ADDING COLOR:

Color can be added to the back-up by fretting the 5th string with the left thumb while playing the Forward Roll with the right hand. This technique can be used with each chord in a song, or it can be used only occassionally to embellish the back-up.

NOTE: Two Forward Roll patterns can be combined by simply playing the same right hand fingering twice; or the right fingers can continue rolling in the same direction for two measures, (16 eighth notes). The following chord progression demonstrates a commonly used two measure pattern of the Forward Roll, for each chord.

CHORD PROGRESSION
using the Forward Roll
(two measure pattern)

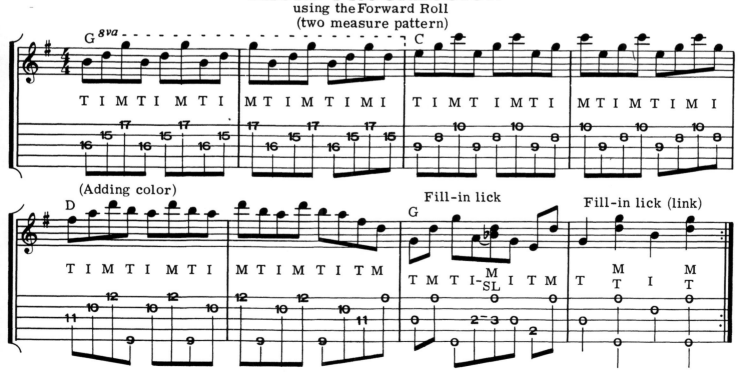

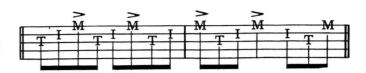

SYNCOPATED VARIATION of the Forward Roll:

The rhythm of the Forward Roll pattern is frequently syncopated to give the back-up a ragtime
effect. The following pattern is a commonly used back-up pattern when the chords are played
up-the-neck. This pattern can be used for each chord for an entire back-up arrangement, or
it can be combined with other back-up patterns. (Notice that this is a two measure pattern,
or the equivalent of two roll patterns.) [pause for the ♩]

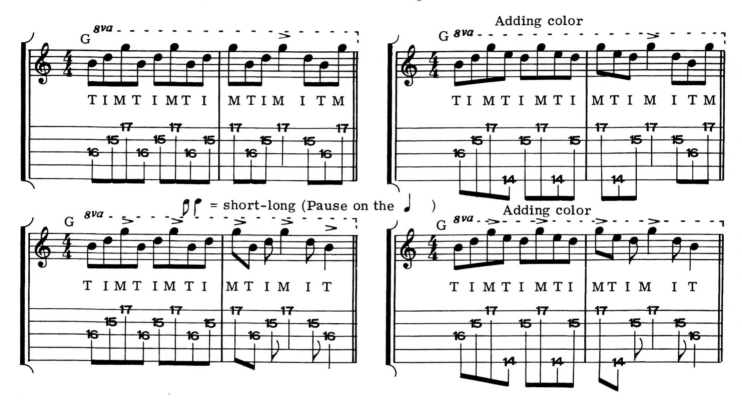

CHORD PROGRESSION
using the Forward Roll with syncopation

2. THE BACKWARD ROLL:

As is true of all of the Standard Roll patterns, this pattern can be used while holding any chord with the left hand. In up-the-neck back-up, the backward roll is frequently used to add color to the back-up. (Many people find it uncomfortable to fret the 5th string with their thumb, and prefer, instead, to add color by playing 6th and 7th chords with the Backward Roll.)

NOTE: to add color to the back-up, the 6th or 7th chord is substituted for the major chord by the same name, i.e. i.e. C7 would be substituted for C; G7 for G; etc.

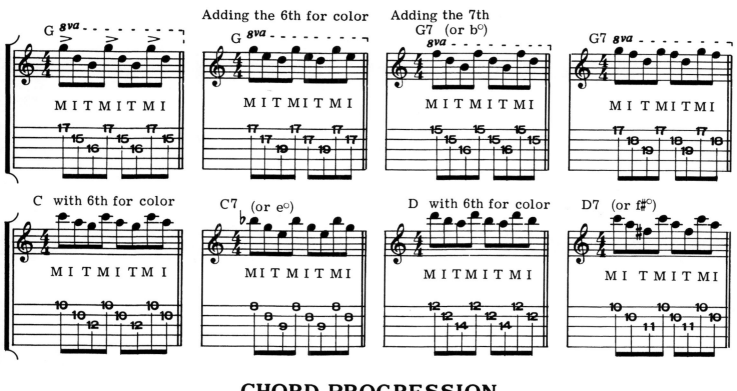

CHORD PROGRESSION
using the Backward Roll for Color

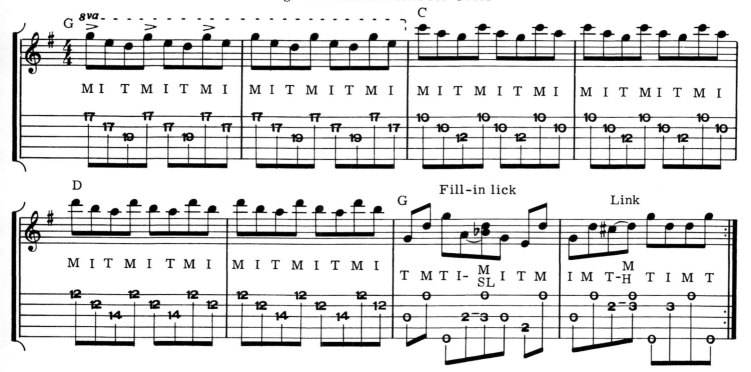

3. THE MIXED ROLL--"D" POSITION PATTERN:

This form of the Mixed Roll pattern is a very popular back-up roll pattern for chords held in the "D" position. (The basic alternating thumb pattern is used primarily with the deeper tones of the banjo.) Notice when playing through the following examples, that this is the same pattern as the Mixed Roll Variation commonly used for the C and D chords played on the deeper tones of the banjo, (p.59). When playing through each of the following patterns, hold the full chord position with the left hand, and use the left ring finger as a pivot between the 3rd and 4th strings as required by the pattern.

THIS PATTERN CAN BE USED FOR ANY CHORD HELD IN THE "D" POSITION!

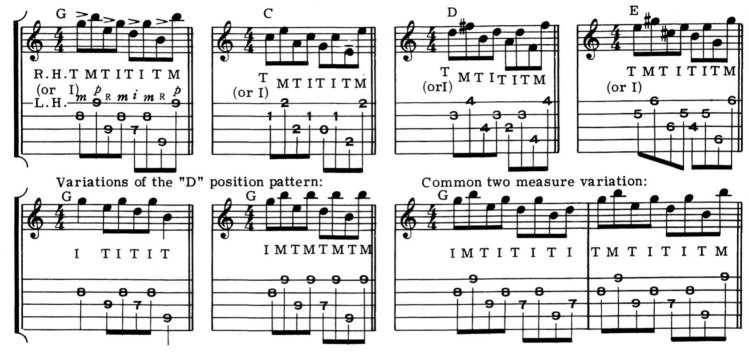

Variations of the "D" position pattern:

Common two measure variation:

CHORD PROGRESSION
using the Mixed Roll--"D" Position Pattern

90

4. THE FORWARD-REVERSE ROLL:

This pattern is an extremely popular up-the-neck back-up pattern which can be used with ANY chord. It is also the only roll pattern that uses the open 5th string with any frequency. However, many people also prefer to fret the 5th string with the left thumb when playing this pattern. (Use your ear to determine when to fret the 5th string and when to leave it open. Basically, it is optional.) The right thumb can pick the 3rd, 4th, or 5th string when this pattern is played, so the 5th string can also be avoided.

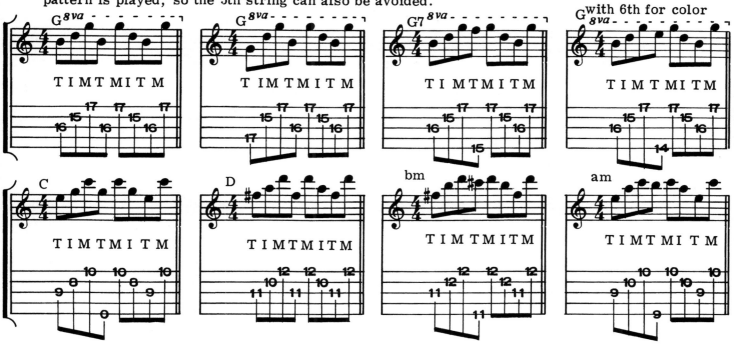

CHORD PROGRESSION PATTERN: (Passing Chords)

The Forward-Reverse Roll Pattern is used by many current banjo players to travel through passing chords, leading the music from one chord to another chord. The pattern is played for the first chord of the pattern, when it is used in back-up, even though the left hand travels through several different chords. Notice in the following examples, that while the left hand moves from one chord position to the next, the right hand is simply playing the Forward-Reverse Roll Pattern twice. (Each pattern=2 measures or rolls)

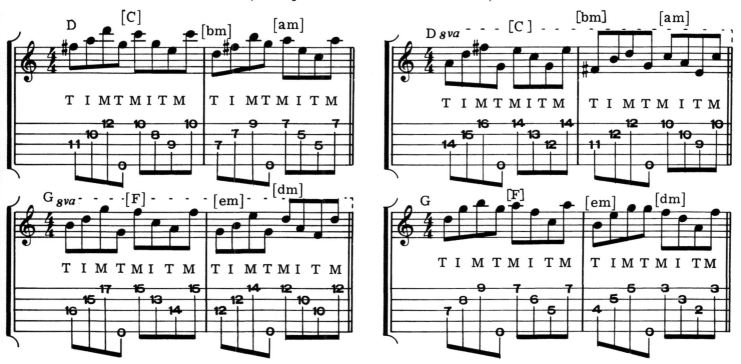

The following chord progressions can be played effectively as back-up, using the Forward-Reverse Roll as the primary back-up pattern for each chord. The first chord progression uses a common two measure pattern, (the first roll begins with either the 3rd or 4th string, and the second roll begins with the 5th string), for each chord.

CHORD PROGRESSION
using the Forward-Reverse Roll

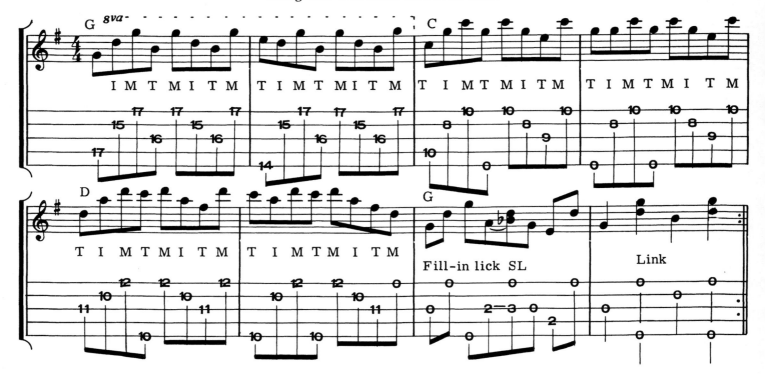

CHORD PROGRESSION
using the Forward-Reverse Roll

This roll pattern is often used as the primary back-up pattern for songs which change chords frequently. The following progression can be played as back-up for the song, "Salty Dog". (The final D chord uses passing chords to lead the music back to the G chord.)

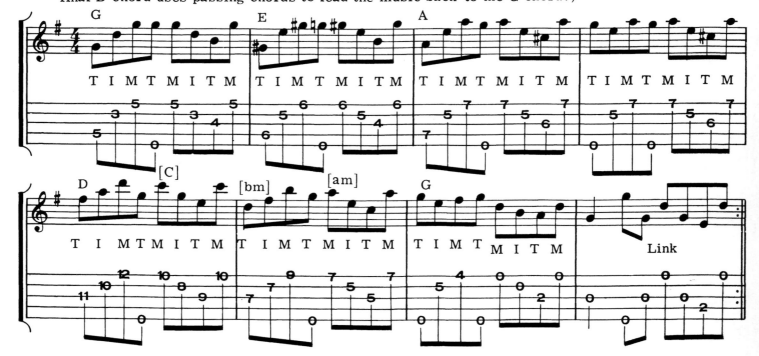

UP-THE-NECK FILL-IN LICKS

The following section is concerned with specific up-the-neck licks which can add excitement, energy, and drive to the back-up. These licks can be combined with one another according to the chords of a song to form a back-up arrangement, or they can be used with any of the other back-up styles and techniques discussed previously, including those played with the deeper tones of the banjo.

The licks on the following pages are divided into three categories:
1. PATTERNS which can be played for ANY chord
2. SINGLE STRING Scruggs-style licks
3. LICKS FOR ONLY SPECIFIC CHORDS

1. <u>PATTERNS</u>: The licks belonging to the first category of up-the-neck licks, can be used to play ANY major chord. Each lick is actually a pattern which works from one of the three major chord positions: F Position, D Position, or Barre Position. By holding a chord in the designated position with the left hand, and following the pattern given for the desired lick, each lick should easily be applied to any chord. For example, Lick #1 on the following page can be played for any major chord by working from the "F" Position of the chord:

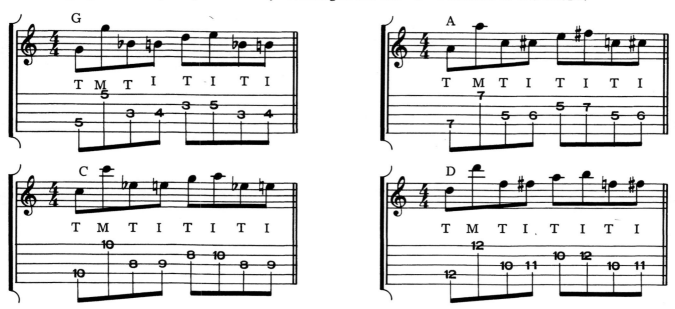

2. <u>SINGLE-STRING</u> <u>Scruggs-style</u> <u>licks</u>: The licks belonging to the second category of licks are generally played for the chords given in the examples. However, these licks can also be used for other major chords by applying the method described for the licks in the above category.

3. <u>LICKS</u> <u>FOR</u> <u>ONLY</u> <u>SPECIFIC</u> <u>CHORDS</u>: The third category of up-the-neck licks offers examples for only the G, C, and D chords. Unlike the licks belonging to the first two categories, these licks frequently involve picking the open 5th string.

The licks belonging to the first two categories are generally used as back-up for <u>medium tempo vocals</u>. (They can be used for any song played at a tempo which allows you to play the licks accurately.) When the banjo is accompanying another instrument, these licks are usually reserved for the pauses in the melody line, (for use as fill-in licks to embellish the pauses). The licks belonging to the third category are used with songs played at any tempo, and are very effective for adding drive to songs played at a very <u>fast</u> <u>tempo</u>. Although they should be used with care when accompanying another instrument, these licks are often able to provide a counter melody to the instrument playing the melody--especially the fiddle.

NOTE: Many of these licks require the right hand to pick the <u>same</u> string two or more times in a row. The <u>suggested</u> right hand fingering is based upon common practice, and may help make these licks easier to play.

PATTERNS

Although each of the following examples is given only for the G chord, each lick can be played for ANY CHORD simply by holding the left hand in the designated moveable chord position for the desired chord, when the lick begins. (The fingers may move out of the chord position as the lick is being played.)

"F" POSITION LICKS

To begin each lick, hold the chord in its "F" Position with the left hand .
NOTE: To hear how each pattern sounds when it is used in back-up, either play the pattern twice without pausing, or follow it with the forward roll pattern:

NOTE: (Left hand fingering is indicated above the musical notation.)

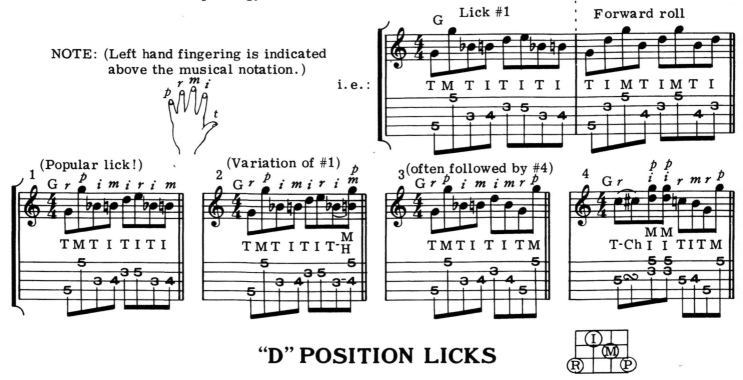

"D" POSITION LICKS

To begin each lick, hold the chord in its "D" Position with the left hand. To hear how each pattern sounds when it is used in back-up, either play the pattern twice without pausing, or follow it with the "D" Position Mixed Roll:

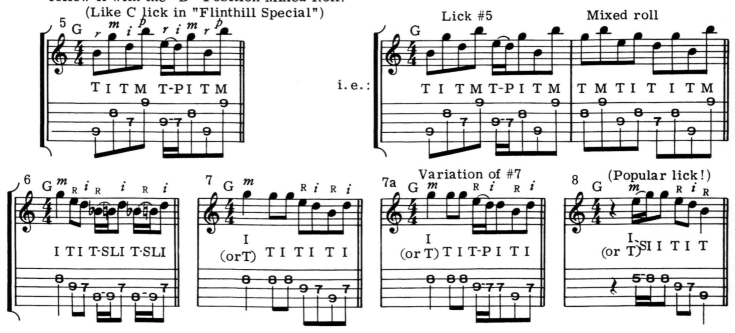

94

"BARRE" POSITION LICKS

The following licks are used to <u>embellish</u> songs played at a medium tempo, <u>and</u> they are also used as <u>primary back-up patterns</u> for slow songs, in the same manner the roll patterns are used. To begin each lick, hold the chord in its "barre" position with the left index finger, (or with the left hand fingering you prefer). (#9, #10, & #11 use only <u>partial chords</u>, so only the first two strings need to be fretted with the left hand.) To hear how each pattern sounds when it is used as back-up, play each pattern twice without pausing.

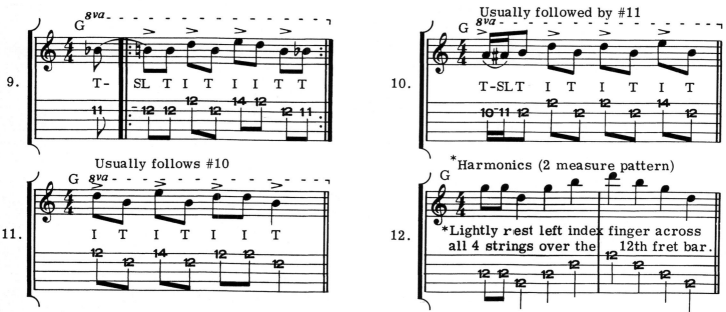

NOTE: When the above licks are used as the primary back-up patterns for slow songs, many variations are possible. (see p.204 for slow song back-up)

<u>LICKS USING MORE THAN ONE CHORD POSITION</u>:

To play the following lick, the left hand moves from the "F" Position of the chord to the "D" position of the same chord. (This back-up lick is often followed by the 'D" position Mixed Roll.)

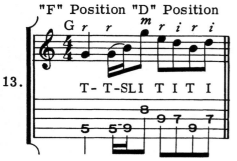

As with all of these up-the-neck licks, this lick can be played as back-up for any major chord by holding the correct chord positions for the chord: (Because the C chord is located 5 frets higher than the G chord, each note of this lick is played 5 frets higher for the C chord):

i.e.

The following lick is one of the most active and most popular of the Scruggs-style Fill-In Licks. It can be used for ANY chord by playing the correct chord positions for the chord with the left hand. To play this lick, the left hand begins in the "F" position of the chord, slides to the "D" Position, moves to the "barre" position, and returns to the "D" Position of the chord. (This lick is often followed by a fill-in lick played on the deeper tones of the banjo.)

for C:

SCRUGGS-STYLE
LICKS USING SINGLE STRINGS

The following licks involve playing the first string several times in a row. Instead of holding full chord positions with the left hand, the left fingers are required to "walk" the strings. The chord positions, however, should be used as reference points for playing these licks.

If you will count the number of times the 1st string is picked when first playing through the following licks, it will be easier to play them with the correct timing. The first note of each lick below belongs to the "F" Position of the chord. (Use the "F" Position as a reference point for playing this lick for any chord.)

NOTE: each lick is a two measure pattern. (An eighth rest (∤) is often substituted for the 1st note.)

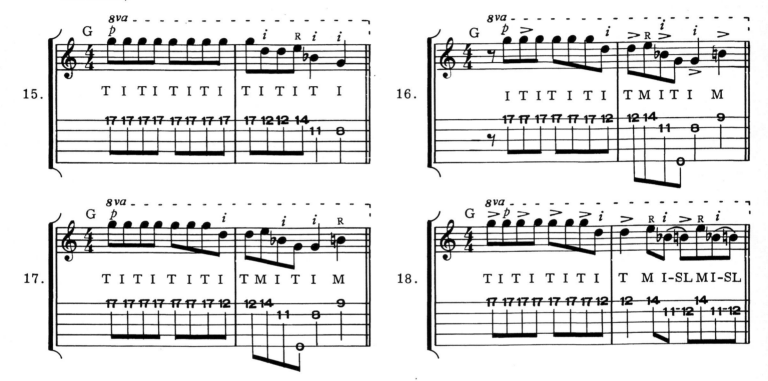

The following licks are used frequently in back-up to draw a break to a close. To hear how each lick should sound as back-up, follow each lick with the following up-the-neck lick:
(#18 (above) is also used as an ending lick.)

NOTE: notice that #18, #19 and #20 use the same lick pattern for the second measure.

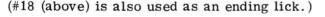

Begins with "Barre" position
(for reference)

Begins with "F" Position
(for reference)

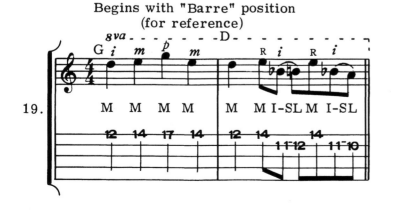

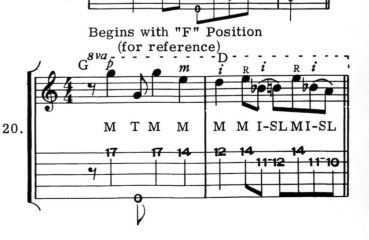

begins with "Barre" position
(for reference)

begins with "F" Position
(for reference)

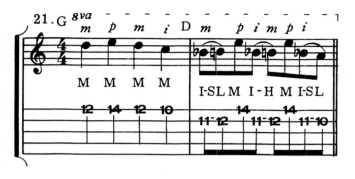 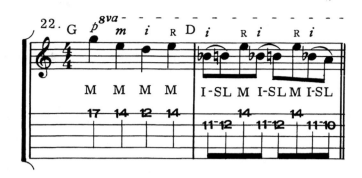

The following licks are used in the lead break for the tune "Foggy Mountain Special". These licks have been used as back-up licks for many songs played at any tempo, but they are primarily used for slower paced songs, because they are difficult to play at a rapid tempo, (i.e. "Hot Corn, Cold Corn" and "Take this Hammer".)

The following lick is actually a combination of several of the above licks. It can be used as an ending lick for songs which use a G (one measure)-D (one measure)-G chord ending, (i.e. "Your Love Is Like A flower", "Hard Ain't It Hard", "Nine Pound Hammer", "Wreck Of The Old 97", etc.) The lick consists of 4 measures; the 5th measure is included to demonstrate how the link connects one verse (or break) with the next verse.

UP-THE-NECK LICKS
FOR SPECIFIC CHORDS

The following back-up licks can be used only for the chord indicated, (because they include
the open 5th string). These licks can be combined with any of the back-up techniques discussed
in this book. They can be used along with back-up played on the deeper tones of the banjo,
(i.e. as fill-in licks, or embellishment), or they can be used in an up-the-neck back-up arrange—
ment. These licks can also be combined with one another, and are frequently used in this
manner to back-up songs played at a very <u>fast</u> tempo. They are effective as back-up for any
lead instrument and for vocals. (If the fiddle is playing an extra long break, or if it plays
several lead breaks, these licks can be used to add life to the usual fiddle back-up played on
the deeper tones of the banjo.)

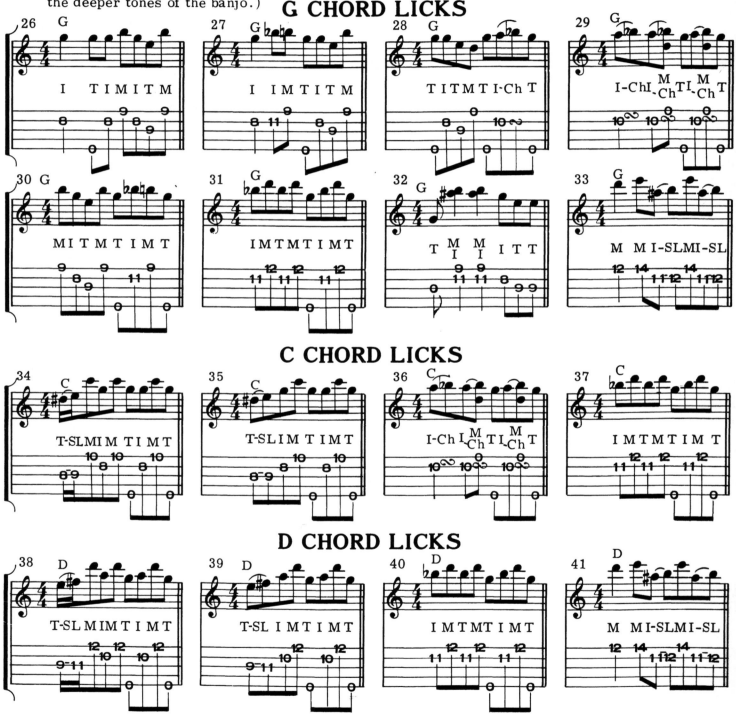

NOTE: G #26, 27, 28 and 30 can also be used for em.
NOTE: G #29 and #31 can also be used for C and D chords.

The up-the-neck fill-in licks can be used as fill-in licks along with any of the other techniques and licks discussed so far in the book, or they can be combined with one another to form a back-up arrangement. Each of the following chord progressions can be used as back-up for the songs listed on p. 18. The number appearing above each measure corresponds to the number of that specific lick in the preceding discussion on up-the-neck fill-in licks.

CHORD PROGRESSION
combining Scruggs-style Back-Up techniques

CHORD PROGRESSION
combining up-the-neck fill-in licks, only

NOTE: DON'T PAUSE BETWEEN LICKS when playing through this progression. Although you know that the back-up is built from licks, this should not be evident to the listener.

SCRUGGS-STYLE BACK-UP
SONGS
UP-THE-NECK BACK-UP

The following back-up arrangements demonstrate the use of all of the back-up techniques discussed in the section on Scruggs-style back-up played up-the-neck. The back-up arrangements for each song appear in order, from using the basic roll patterns as accompaniment, to playing back-up with the more advanced licks. Each of the arrangements can be used as back-up for a complete song by repeating the arrangement over and over for the duration of the song, or the arrangements can be combined simply by going directly from one back-up arrangement to the next without pausing. The link is used to connect the arrangements. Due to the constant activity of the banjo when it is playing several of the up-the-neck licks in a row, the arrangements which use these licks should generally be reserved either for back-up for a vocalist or for the fiddle. Keep in mind when playing through these, that the most advanced arrangement is not always the most effective. Many times, the simplest back-up is the most effective accompaniment!

NOTE: A back-up arrangement for each of these songs also appears in the section on Scruggs-style back-up played with the deep tones of the banjo. The following arrangements may also be combined with those arrangements.

NOTE: The number appearing with each lick corresponds to the number of that lick in the examples given in the discussions for using up-the-neck licks, (from pages 93-98).

NOTE: When playing through these arrangements, the left hand should hold full (all four strings) chord positions.

NOTE: The right hand should be located in the "Y" Position, well away from the bridge, --very close to the fingerboard, when the back-up is played up-the-neck.

WABASH CANNONBALL

(a lead arrangement is on page 33)

BACK-UP--using standard ROLL PATTERNS up-the-neck; Hold chords with the left hand!

NOTE: The right hand should play this arrangement from the Y position--near the neck.

NOTE: See pages: 34-38, 75, 102-106, 207-208 for other back-up arrangements for this tune.

II. BACK-UP: ADDING COLOR to the roll patterns, & using different positions of the same chords:

NOTE: When playing the forward roll, accent the 1st string.

III. BACK-UP--ADDING PASSING TONES: (up-the neck)

Hold full chord positions with the left hand when playing this arrangement.

IV. BACK-UP-- COMBINING ROLL PATTERNS AND LICKS FROM pp.86-98.

BACK-UP: USING LICKS (up-the-neck) FOR SPECIFIC CHORDS (p.98)

FOR PRACTICE: Substitute other up-the-neck licks into the above back-up arrangement for the correct chords.

VI. BACK-UP--COMBINING UP-THE-NECK LICKS: The # corresponds to the example of the lick from pp. 93-98.

JOHN HARDY
BACK-UP

A lead break for this song can be found on p. 39.
BACK-UP: USING THE FORWARD ROLL AND FILL-IN LICKS:

NOTE: For other back-up arrangements, see pages: 40-44, 76, 108-111.

II. BACK-UP: USING ROLL PATTERNS, & ADDING COLOR:

108

III. BACK-UP--USING SUBSTITUTE CHORDS & CURRENT POPULAR FILL-IN LICKS:

IV. BACK-UP--USING ROLL PATTERNS, PASSING TONES, & LICK #13 (from p.95)
WITH RHYTHMIC EMBELLISHMENT:

V. BACK-UP--USING LICKS (up-the-neck) FOR SPECIFIC CHORDS: (see p.98)

NEW RIVER TRAIN

The following back-up arrangement is especially effective behind a vocalist. However, it can also be used as back-up behind another instrument. This arrangement uses the Forward Roll and the Mixed Roll patterns for the basis of the back-up, and uses passing tones to lead the music from one chord into a new chord. (Notice that the Forward Roll is used for the "F" position chords, while the Mixed Roll is used for the "D" position chords. Although there is no rule governing which rolls should be used when, this arrangement demonstrates a common usage of these patterns.) See page 79 for lead arrangement.

I. BACK-UP--USING UP-THE-NECK ROLL PATTERNS AND PASSING TONES:

NOTE: Other back-up arrangements can be found on pages: 80, 113, 114.

BACK-UP

(A lead arr. can be found on p.79)

The following back-up arrangement combines the roll patterns with the up-the-neck embellishment patterns from pp.93-98. (The number corresponds to the example of the lick on those pages.) For practice, try substituting other licks from those pages for these licks, according to the correct chords in the song. (For example, you might substitute lick #13 for lick #8 in the 3rd measure below).

II. BACK-UP--USING ROLL PATTERNS & UP-THE-NECK LICKS:

The following arrangement is based upon the back-up arrangement on the preceding page. However, several of the licks from pp. 93-98 have been changed. The purpose of this is to demonstrate that not only can the same roll patterns and licks be used as back-up for many different songs, but also, many different roll patterns and licks can be used as back-up for the same song, as long as they are used for the correct chords to the song.

III. BACK-UP: SUBSTITUTING LICKS:

WRECK OF THE OLD 97
BACK-UP

A lead break for this tune can be found on p. 83. The following back-up arrangement consists of a combination of various roll patterns played by the right hand, while chords are held in up-the-neck positions by the left hand.

I. BACK-UP: UP-THE-NECK ROLL PATTERNS:

NOTE: Other back-up arrangements for this tune can be found on pages: 84, 116, 117. (The arrangements are written so that you can go directly from one arrangement to another without pausing. The link connects the arrangements.)

The following back-up arrangement adds rhythmic embellishment to the roll patterns used in the back-up arrangement on the previous page (p. 115). Keep in mind when playing through these patterns, that ♪♩ = short-long rhythm, (pause after the quarter note (♩), and that 𝄾 means to rest or pause for the duration of an eighth note (♪).

II. BACK-UP: RHYTHMIC EMBELLISHMENT--up-the-neck back-up

III. BACK-UP--COMBINING up-the-neck ROLL PATTERNS AND LICKS: (the left hand chord positions are indicated above the measures along with the chord symbols. Hold full chords -- all four strings--with the left hand.)

LONG JOURNEY HOME
BACK-UP

I. <u>BACK-UP</u>--the following arrangement combines vamping, roll patterns played up-the-neck, and fill-in licks played on the deeper tones. (see lead arr. p. 81)

*ending: G [to end song play <u>immediately</u> <u>after</u> D lick above.]

NOTE: See p. 82 for another back-up arrangement for this tune.

EAST VIRGINIA BLUES
BACK-UP

A lead arrangement for this tune can be found on p.77. The following back-up arrangement is based upon vamping patterns, and uses the up-the-neck embellishing patterns and licks to fill-in the pauses in the melody lines. For practice substitute other licks appearing throughout this book for the fill-in licks below... (NOTE: each fill-in lick below is played for a G chord).

I. BACK-UP--vamping and up-the neck fill-in licks:

NOTE: See page 78 for another back-up arrangement for this tune.

ENDINGS

Often the final job falling upon the banjo player when he is playing back-up, is that of providing an effective ending for the song. This is true not only for instrumental songs where the banjo takes the final lead break, but also for singing songs. The following examples are commonly used by many banjo players to end songs which are played in the key of G. (Several of these endings have also been demonstrated with the songs throughout the book, for keys other than the Key of G.) NOTE: The "vocal" and "instrumental" designations are merely to serve as guidelines based upon the way these endings are commonly used; however, each ending may actually serve in either capacity.

VOCAL ENDINGS:

These endings are played for the last chord of the song.

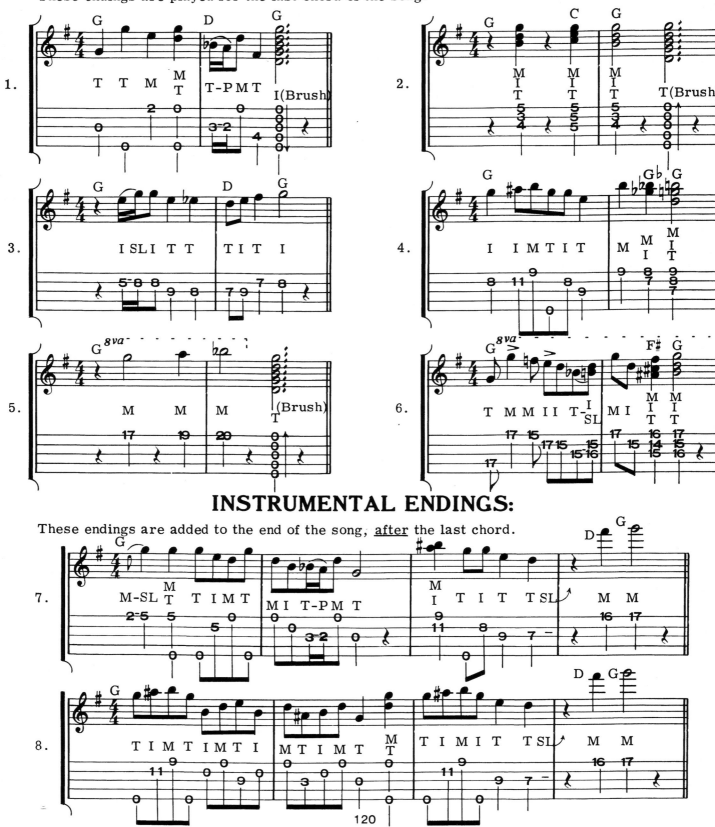

INSTRUMENTAL ENDINGS:

These endings are added to the end of the song, after the last chord.

GUIDELINES FOR USING BACK-UP STYLES AND TECHNIQUES

The following suggestions are some guidelines you can follow for various types of lead breaks, until you have developed your own feeling for back-up.

VOCALS: (singing songs)

Hard Driving Songs: (fast) These songs often sound best when backed up with steady, continuous licks, giving them a sense of forward movement. The fill-in licks (see p.28-29) are often combined according to the chords of the song when the back-up is played with the deep tones of the banjo; the licks on p. 98 are often combined for up-the-neck back-up. The roll patterns, especially the forward roll and the forward-reverse roll, are also very effective for up-the-neck back-up, particularly when color is added to the chords with the 5th string. Vamping is also very effective as back-up for fast vocals.
REMEMBER: the licks and roll patterns must correspond with the chords in the song.

Slow Songs: Playing licks and roll patterns high on the fingerboard often provides effective back-up for slow songs. The licks using partial chord positions (see p.204-6) are effective in adding a lilt or a bounce to the overall effect of the song. The Mixed roll pattern is frequently used to back-up slow songs played on the deep tones of the banjo, while the forward roll is an effective back-up pattern when it is played up-the-neck for slow songs. Triplets also provide an effective style of back-up, particularly for very slow songs, (see p.214).

Medium Tempo Songs: Any style of back-up can be used for these songs, and the banjo player can generally have a lot of fun accompanying them. There is usually enough time to play all over the fingerboard with various back-up licks and harmonies, yet, at the same time, the song has plenty of energy and drive to keep the back-up exciting. Active back-up played with rolls and licks is one of the most popular forms of back-up for medium speed vocals. The key to effective back-up is always to LISTEN to the lead and to the other back-up instruments and try to find a style that works well with what they are doing.

INSTRUMENTAL LEAD BREAKS:

Guitar: One method is to keep the banjo simple by playing rhythm and chords. Simply vamping chords high on the fingerboard, and using a few passing tones for embellishment can be very effective. Scruggs-style licks, especially those discussed under 1st-5th fret area (see p.62), can also be effective for guitar back-up, particularly when the guitar is playing a fiddle tune. Because the pitch range and the timbre (tone quality) of the guitar are similar to those of the banjo, the banjo player has to be careful not to compete with the guitar. Fiddle tune back-up is effective on the deep tones because it creates a counter-melody which compliments the lead. However, when in doubt, vamping is best.

Dobro: Basically the same techniques are used to back up the dobro that are used to back-up the guitar. (Vamping with the use of passing tones for embellishment is usually the preferred style).

Fiddle: Two techniques are frequently used behind fiddle breaks:

    1. Scruggs-style back-up played on the deep tones of the banjo, (pp.56-73) is effective in balancing the higher tones of the fiddle. Vamping is frequently used along with this style of back-up for fiddle tunes, where virtually every note played by the fiddle is a melody note.

    2. Up-the-neck Scruggs licks for specific chords (see p.98) are often used to create a counter-melody in the same tonal range the fiddle is playing. (For more on fiddle back-up, see p.184).

Mandolin: Two techniques are frequently used to back-up the mandolin:

    1. As in back-up for the fiddle, the most commonly used style is Scruggs-style back-up played on the deep tones of the banjo, (pp.56-73). These licks balance the high tones of the mandolin and at the same time give the song a feeling of forward motion. If the song is played at a very fast tempo, the fill-in licks (p.28-29) are frequently combined according to the chords of the song to provide the back-up.

    2. If the mandolin is playing a lot of tremelo and chords, as opposed to single strings, the song may sound less cluttered if the banjo vamps chords, playing rhythm.

Bass: If the bass player takes a lead break, the banjo player often brushes or vamps the correct chord once on the downbeat of each measure. (Generally all of the instruments will do this together.) Silence on the part of all of the other instruments, including the banjo, is also a form of back-up used for a bass lead break. The effect of all of the instruments entering at the end of the break can be very dynamic.

COMMON LEAD PROCEDURE
FOR A BLUEGRASS BAND

A bluegrass band normally consists of four or more musicians playing acoustic (non-electric) instruments which generally include guitar, bass, banjo, mandolin, fiddle, and/or dobro, (and occasionally harmonica). The following guidelines are ONLY suggestions which are based upon the procedure followed by many bluegrass bands. There are no rules governing back-up or the procedure used by a band. These guidelines are simply provided to answer questions which may arise when someone is new to playing back-up. These are simply a base from which to begin.

VOCALS: (singing songs) A vocal song normally opens with one of the instruments playing through the melody of the verse before the vocalist begins singing. (The introduction may also be shortened, so that it includes only the last line of the verse, for example.) The vocalist sings one (or two) verses plus the refrain of the song, and then an instrument usually plays a break, (which is normally the melody to the verse rather than to the refrain). Then the vocalist sings the next verse and refrain. If an instrument plays a break after the last verse of the song, the vocalist will sing only the refrain and the song will be ended. However, normally the song is ended after the last verse and refrain. Vocal endings are usually played with the last chord of the song, rather than added as a tag ending, (added to the last chord.) (The examples in the following section of songs demonstrate vocal endings.) Also see p.120.

INSTRUMENTALS: The procedure for playing this type of song is quite varied, not only from group to group, but also from song to song. The instruments may take turns, each playing through the melody once; each instrument may play through the song twice, (as is often the procedure with "Foggy Mountain Breakdown"); or each instrument may play through the song several times in a row before the next instrument takes his break, (as is often the procedure with "Sally Goodin'"). A song may feature one or all of the instruments in the band, or it may feature only two instruments, such as the banjo and the fiddle, where each one alternates with the other in playing the lead. The last instrument to take a break usually ends the song. (If a song features one particular instrument, it usually begins and ends the song.)

The songs in the following section are designed to demonstrate how the banjo might play a song from beginning to end, along with a bluegrass band. Because this is a book for banjo players, most of the songs begin with a banjo lead break or introduction. However, for practice, you might try inserting the lead in the middle of the song, between two back-up breaks. (The "link" connects the various breaks, so omit the pick-up notes when trying this.)

SONGS

The following songs are arrangements of entire songs, from start to finish. These are intended to demonstrate how all of the back-up styles and techniques discussed throughout this book can be employed for various songs and for various instruments. Each song is written as it might be played on the banjo along with a bluegrass band. For this reason, many different back-up styles and techniques may be used in the same song. Each song begins with a banjo lead break and moves directly into the back-up through a "link". (To hear how the back-up should sound, record the lead break several times in a row without pausing, and then play the song from beginning to end along with your recording.)

Before playing through these songs, analyze them by looking for the various techniques discussed throughout this book. For example:

1. Notice the style of back-up used for the fiddle, the dobro, etc. Compare the fiddle back-up from song to song, noting the similarities and/or the differences in style (area of the fingerboard, etc.).

2. Notice how the back-up for the vocalist increases in intensity, (i.e. through the use of up-the-neck fill-in licks), as each song progresses.

3. Notice that a "link" connects each verse or lead break.

4. Look for the specific roll patterns and licks discussed in each section of the book, and compare the use of these from song to song. (i.e. Notice what roll or lick is used for the C chord in the fiddle back-up from song to song.)

5. Notice that many of the same licks and techniques are used from song to song, regardless of the key in which the song is played. Remember, back-up is accompaniment, which consists of patterns and licks used for the chords to the song. The back-up may be very similar for several different songs, but when played along with the melody for each song, the overall effect of the back-up and the total effect of each song should be quite different from that of the other songs.

NOTE: Each arrangement may include advanced techniques or rhythms. If you have trouble playing these, substitute a roll pattern or vamp the chord for the lick, so that you can play through the song. (Substituting licks and roll patterns for the correct chords is good practice for playing back-up, even if the more advanced patterns don't give you any trouble.)

LITTLE MAGGIE
KEY OF G

Notice that the vamping style of back-up is the foundation for this entire arrangement.

BANJO LEAD:

Medium to fast tempo

VOCAL BACK-UP--vamping and fill-in licks:
(1st verse)

To back-up
(don't pause)

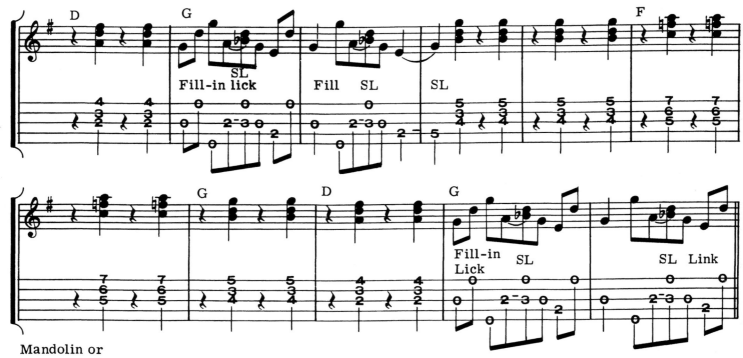

Mandolin or
FIDDLE BACK-UP--Scruggs style on the deep tones of the banjo to balance the high tones of the
fiddle: (This style of back-up adds to the energy of the vamping style used with
the singer.)

VOCAL BACK-UP--vamping plus embellishment to add interest
(2nd verse)

(works from "D" position.)

SL
Embellishment (fill)

Guitar or
DOBRO BACK-UP--combines vamping and Scruggs-style on deep tones (to play counter-melody):

VOCAL BACK-UP: vamping and fill-in licks
(3rd verse)

RED RIVER VALLEY
KEY OF G

The songs: "Red River Valley", "New River Train", "Roll In My Sweet Baby's Arms","She'll Be Comin' Around The Mountain", "Mama Don't Allow", "May I Sleep In Your Barn Tonight Mister?", "Why Don't You Tell Me So?", "When The Saints Go Marchin' In", and "Will You Be Lovin' Another Man?" are built with the same chord progression, (use the same chords at the same time). Therefore, the following back-up can be played for any of these songs when they are played in the Key of G.

129

VOCAL BACK-UP--Scruggs-style on the deeper tones of the banjo: (Each measure contains a back-up pattern.)

FIDDLE OR MANDOLIN BACK-UP--Scruggs-style on the deeper tones of the banjo:

VOCAL BACK-UP--Using up-the-neck Roll Patterns and Licks: (adding drive & energy)

132

DOBRO OR GUITAR BACK-UP: Vamping is the basis, with fill-in licks & embellishing rhythms

VOCAL BACK-UP: primarily a combination of licks (up & down the neck)

NOTE: As you go back through this song, notice that the back-up increases in activity as the song progresses from beginning to end, while at the same time using the style of back-up &/or the area of the fingerboard which best enhances the lead instrument.

FOR PRACTICE:
1. Play the back-up for "New River Train" along with the lead for "Red River Valley", (and vice versa).
2. Play the lead for "Red River Valley" with the capo on the 3rd fret (Key of Bb) into a recorder; remove the capo and play the back-up for "May I Sleep In Your Barn Tonight?" along with your recording.
3. Play the lead for "Red River Valley" with the capo on the 7th fret (Key of D) into a recorder; remove the capo and play the back-up for "She'll Be Coming Around The Mountain" along with it.

JESSE JAMES
KEY OF G

The back-up for this song can also be used as back-up for the songs: "My Little Girl In Tennes-see", "I'm On The Way To Glory Land", &"Cabin In Caroline", for they use the same chord progression.

VOCAL BACK-UP (verse)--Scruggs-style on deeper tones of the banjo:

Up-the-neck embellish-
ment using forward roll

To back-up:
(Don't Pause)

(refrain)--up-the-neck roll patterns:

137

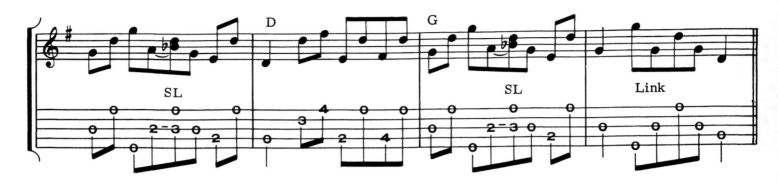

FIDDLE OR MANDOLIN BACK-UP--using the deep tones of the banjo:

*NOTE: An extra link is often needed before the vocalist begins singing after an instrumental
break.

VOCAL BACK-UP--up-the-neck rolls plus embellishing licks:

(refrain)--deep tones with up-the-neck licks for embellishment:

139

FIDDLE BACK-UP--up-the-neck licks for specific chords.(p.98)

141

NOTE ON ENDING: The banjo often brings singing songs (vocals) to a close with this ending
Notice that it is played for the final G chord immediately after the D chord!

BURY ME BENEATH THE WILLOW
KEY OF G

The following back-up arrangements can also be played as back-up for: "Wreck of the Old 97",
"Your Love Is Like A Flower", "Hard Ain't It Hard", & "If I Should Wander Back Tonight".

INTRODUCTION: Banjo lead-in--(This is not a complete banjo break)(see page 145 for complete break)

Moderate tempo (Not too fast for this arrangement)

Vocal Back-Up--(verse): using the deep tones of the banjo (a frequently used method to begin vocal back-up)

CHORUS(refrain) back-up: (vocal)--vamping chords plus fill-in licks form the back-up for each
refrain--(This style is common when the banjo player sings on the
chorus)

144

BANJO LEAD: (Record this break and play back-up along with your recording). This demonstrates how a banjo lead break is played in the middle of a song.

Also: See discussion on p.204 concerning
VOCAL BACK-UP---Verse: based on lick 9, 10, & 11, page 95: slow song licks (which add bounce).

Passing tones

SL

Link Connects
verse w/refrain

Refrain: vamping and fill-in licks (common back-up style when banjo player sings)

FIDDLE BACK-UP: using the deep tones of the banjo to balance high tones of the fiddle

147

VOCAL BACK-UP--verse: using up-the-neck roll patterns and licks:

Final chorus (refrain) using vamping and fill-in licks plus popular vocal ending

*ENDING: (works from G chord in its "D" position)

*Alternate ending

149

BACK-UP IN ANY KEY

Up to this point, all of the examples in this book have been written for the key of G. The reason for this is that 75% of the songs played on the banjo are (or can be) played in the key of G, and the back-up patterns which are used for that key can easily be applied to any other key. The songs on the following pages demonstrate how back-up can be played in several different keys. Notice that the back-up patterns and techniques are virtually the same from song to song, regardless of the key in which they are played; the songs simply use different chords from one another.

WHAT IS A "KEY"?
The "key" of a song is the tonal center (the note or chord) to which all of the other notes or chords of the song are related. The same song can be played in any key, but different chords will be used, depending upon the key in which the song is played. Most songs begin and end with the chord of the key name.

WHEN AND WHY ARE SONGS PLAYED IN DIFFERENT KEYS?
1. Some songs, (especially instrumentals, and particularly fiddle tunes,) are usually played in a specific key. i.e. "Cotton Patch Rag" is usually played in the Key of C, for this is the key in which fiddle players generally play this song.
2. When a person is singing a song, he will usually sing it in the key that best suits his voice range.
3. Bands often change keys when they are entertaining, using the theory that this helps hold the attention of the audience, (rather than playing an entire set in the same key.)

USING THE CAPO:
When the above occasions arise, the banjo player can often use the capo on the appropriate fret so that he can continue playing as if he were in the key of G, but his banjo will actually be playing the tones of the desired key. The capo is simply placed across the fret where the barre chord named for the key is located...2nd fret=Key of A; 4th fret=Key of B; 5th Fret=Key of C; 7th Fret=Key of D, etc. This works well for songs such as "Salt River" and "Little Maggie" which are often played in the Key of A, but what about the Key of F? Also, the banjo loses the potential for playing back-up on the deeper tones behind the fiddle if the song is played in the Key of C or D with the capo. (Excessive use of the capo can also cause a problem time-wise when a band is performing.)

WHEN PLAYING BACK-UP, HOW DOES THE BANJO PLAYER DETERMINE THE KEY A SONG IS PLAYED IN, WITHOUT BEING TOLD?
A song usually begins with the chord named for the key, and it almost always ends with this chord. i.e. Songs played in the Key of G usually begin and end with the G chord; songs played in the Key of F generally begin and end with the F chord.

WHAT ARE THE PRIMARY CHORDS OF A KEY?
The primary chords of a key are the main chords of the song, (i.e. G, C, and D in the key of G). All of the other chords of the song are related in some manner to one of these chords. If you can find the primary chords for a key, you should easily be able to play back-up in that key, simply by applying the back-up patterns, (i.e. rolls and licks) to those chords.

150

FINDING THE PRIMARY CHORDS OF A KEY:

If you can say the alphabet from A to G, and if you can count on your fingers from one to seven, you should find this fairly easy to use. The musical alphabet is: A B C D E F G A B C...etc. repeated over and over. When a song is played in a certain key, the chords belonging to that key are numbered according to the alphabet, beginning with the key name. For example:

KEY OF G: G   A   B   C   D   E   F   G
            I   ii   iii   IV   V   vi   vii   I

KEY OF C: C   D   E   F   G   A   B   C

KEY OF D: D   E   F   G   A   B   C   D

The PRIMARY CHORDS are the I chord, the IV chord and the V chord in ANY KEY. (Key of G=G, C, &D); (Key of C=C, F, &G): (Key of D=D, G, &A). NOTE: to keep this from becoming confusing, mention of sharps and flats has been omitted. (See p. 14 for explanation of these symbols.)

LOCATING THE PRIMARY CHORDS ON THE BANJO FOR ANY KEY:

First, find the I chord of the key in its "F" Position; then locate the IV chord in its barre position; then find the V chord in its "D" position. This sounds complicated in writing, but it forms an easy to use pattern on the fingerboard of the banjo. If you play through the following pattern, beginning with any chord in the "F" position, you will have the primary chords for the key of the chord you begin with.

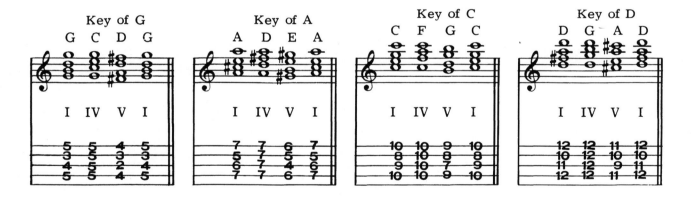

NOTE: The following songs demonstrate how back-up can be played in several different keys, and also in several different tunings. The first few songs are played while the banjo remains in G tuning. However, the 5th string is changed so that it is playing a chord tone of the chord named for the key. This is not necessary for back-up in the key of C, but often helps make playing back-up easier, (if the 5th string is to be used), in other keys.

BATTLE HYMN OF THE REPUBLIC
KEY OF C

Medium tempo

LEAD (for Banjo):

(Primary chords - C, F, and G.)

Begin back-up (do not pause--the link connects the lead break with the back-up.)

MANDOLIN BACK-UP: (Using deep tones of the banjo to counter balance high pitches of the mandolin)

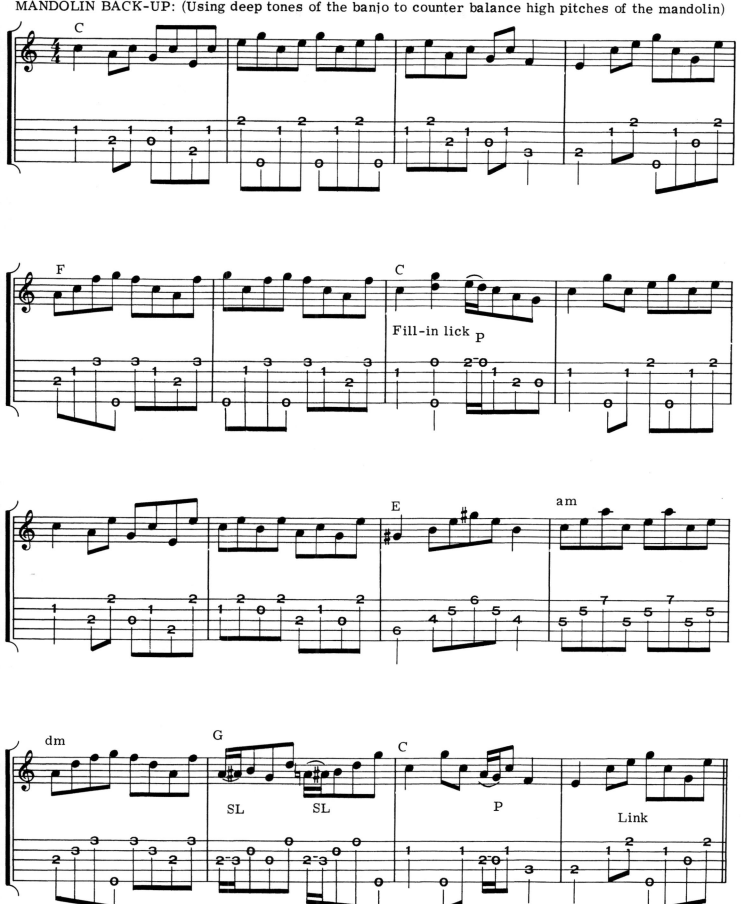

DOBRO OR GUITAR BACK-UP: vamping to avoid competing with the melody

SL   Fill-in lick | Passing tones lead to F

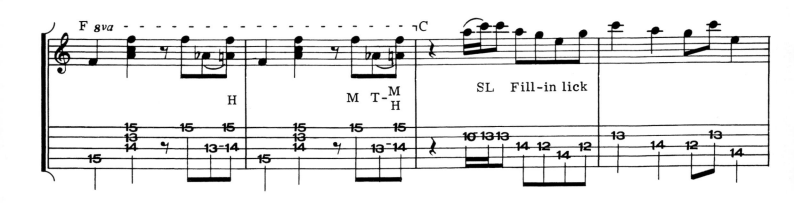

H | M T-M H | SL   Fill-in lick

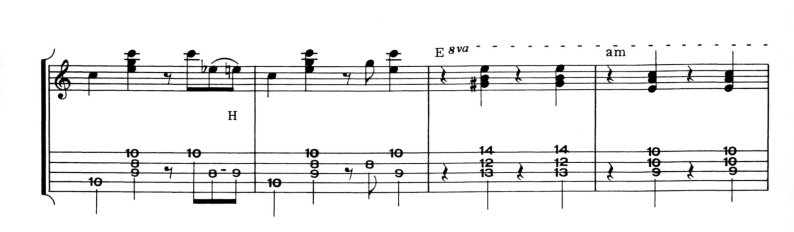

H

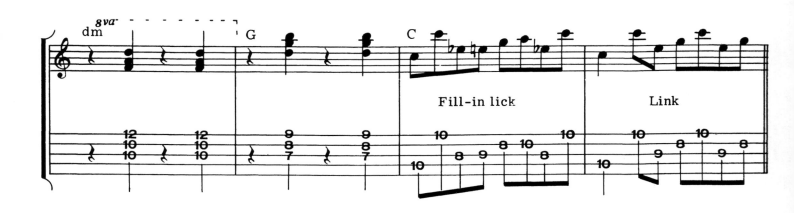

Fill-in lick | Link

FIDDLE BACK-UP: using deep tones to counter balance high tones of the fiddle

NOTE: This arrangement for this tune is written as an instrumental. However, if the back-up is to be played while someone is singing, each of the above back-up arrangements <u>can</u> be used.

BANKS OF THE OHIO
KEY OF C

(Primary chords = C, F and G.)
I, IV, V.

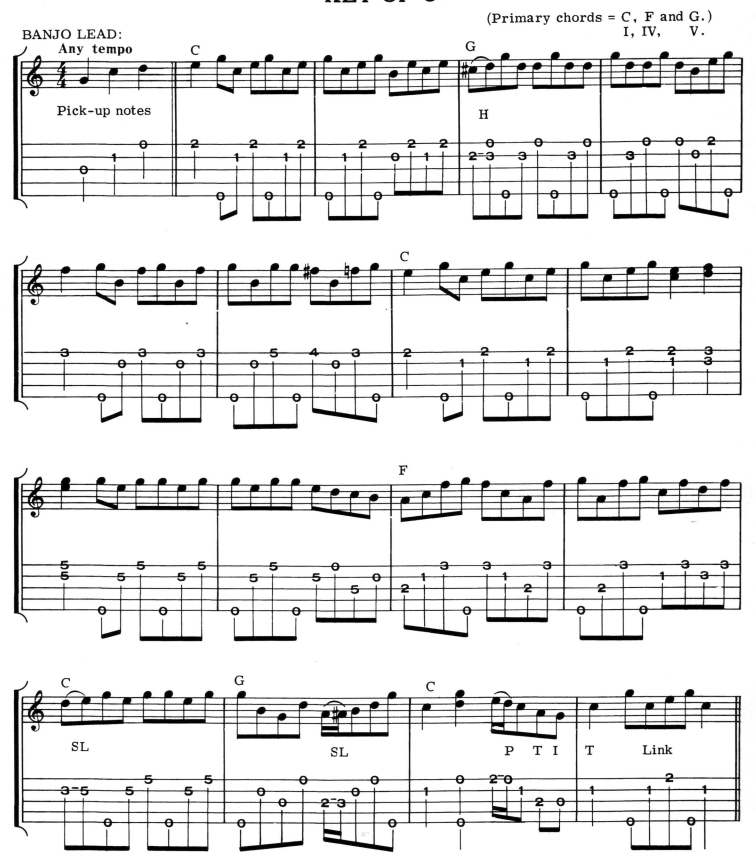

Begin back-up without pausing.

VOCAL BACK-UP--(verse)--using the deep tones of the banjo to begin the song:

Passing tones

SL

SL

SL

Link

Refrain--using roll patterns up-the-neck:

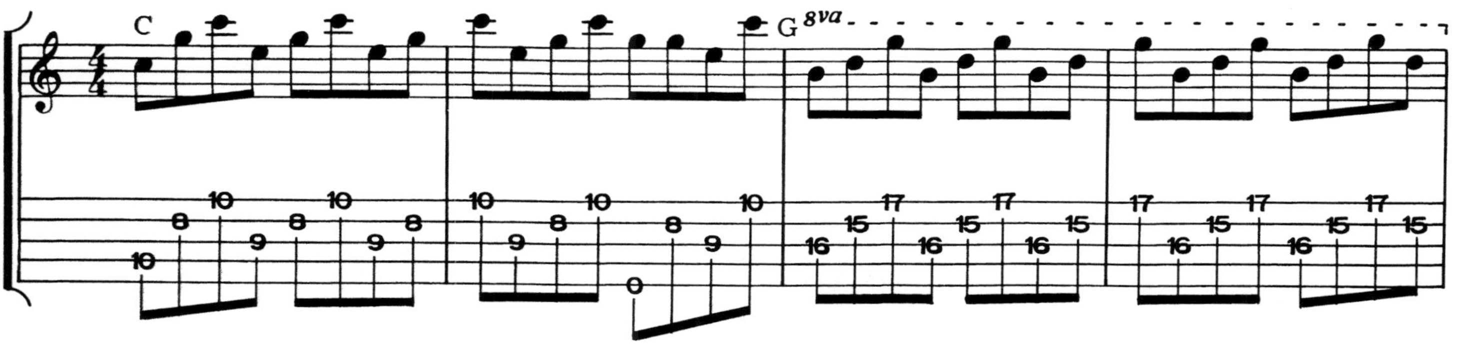

157

Passing tones

INSTRUMENTAL BACK-UP--Vamping: (this can be played as back-up for any instrument)

158

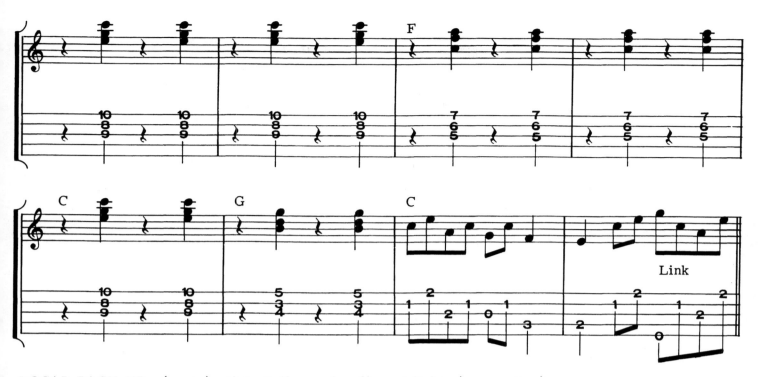

VOCAL BACK-UP--(verse) using up-the-neck rolls and licks: (very active)

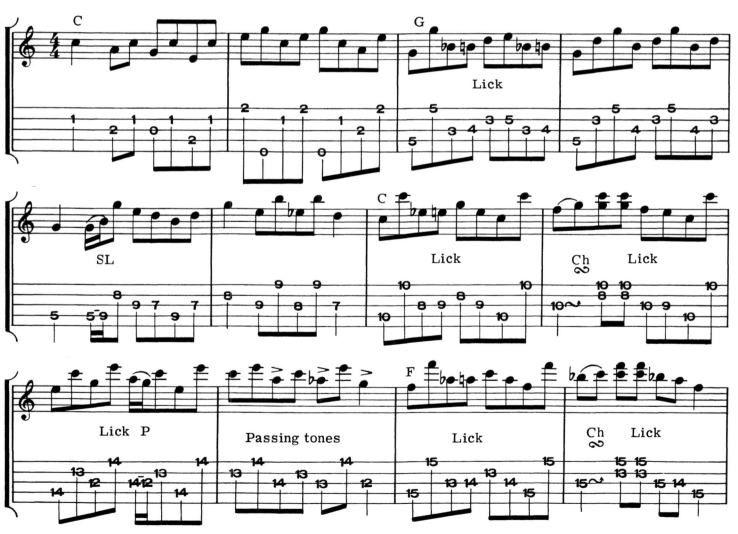

159

Refrain--deep tones with up-the-neck licks

*NOTE: Notice that the ending used above (in the key of C for the C chord) is the same one used in "Bury Me Beneath The Willow" (in the key of G for the G chord).

JOHN HENRY
KEY OF D

G tuning--tune 5th string (to A)

Tune the 5th string to sound like the 1st string, 7th fret; (place the 5th string capo on the 2nd fret;)(don't alter the other strings.)

BANJO LEAD:

161

Proceed to back-up

The following back-up arrangements use fairly basic back-up techniques.
INSTRUMENTAL BACK-UP--using the basic vamping rhythm for the chords to the song:

INSTRUMENTAL BACK-UP--Because this song stays on one chord (D) much of the time, it enables the banjo to effectively play a counter-melody involving a fairly active accompaniment along with any instrument, without competing with the melody.

* Ending: substitute this measure for the link to end the song.

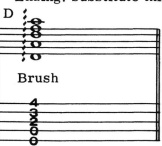

*NOTE: Repeat the lead break or any back-up break, or end the song as follows:

SHE'LL BE COMIN' AROUND THE MOUNTAIN
KEY OF D

G Tuning with 5th string tuned to A.

Raise 5th string pitch to sound like 1st string, 7th fret (A);   (place 5th string capo on 2nd fret.)

(Leave all other strings alone.)

BANJO LEAD:

Primary chords = D G and A.

                                                   I   IV   V

VOCAL BACK-UP-- using roll patterns on deep tones of the banjo (hold chords with left hand)

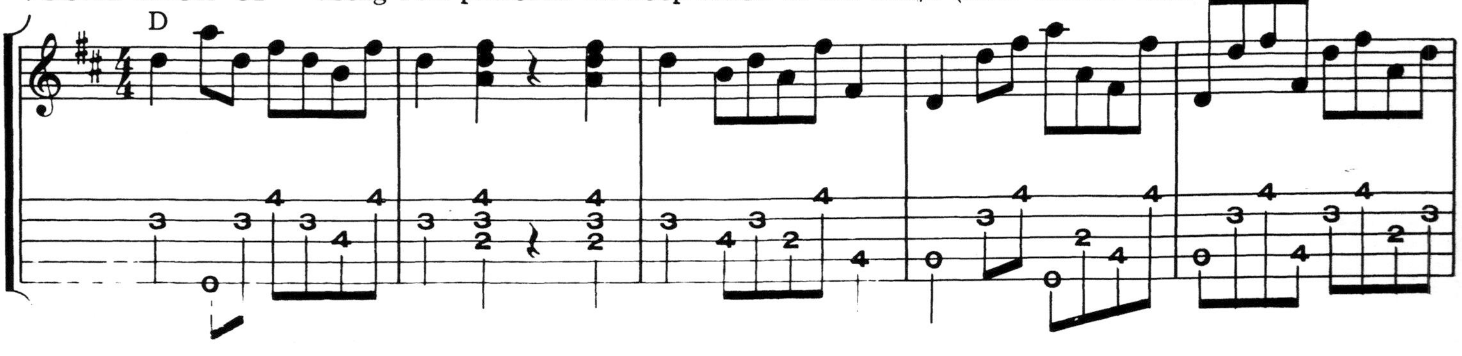

164

GUITAR (OR DOBRO) BACK-UP--vamping and fill-in licks (for pauses in melody line at cadences)

Fill-in lick

SL Lick

...Fill--using the found roll...

165

Passing tones

VOCAL BACK-UP--begins with deep tones and moves up-the-neck..increasing intensity of the song

SL   Link

Fill-in using forward roll up-the-neck
(embellishment of deeper tones)

Passing tones (taking
back-up up the neck)

Lick

Passing tones

Lick P

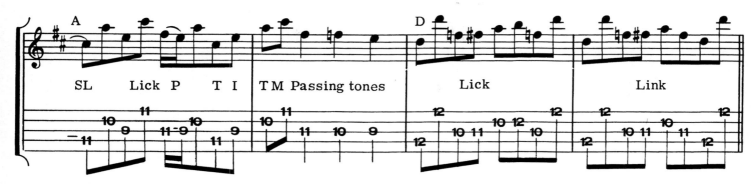

FIDDLE (OR MANDOLIN) BACK-UP--using deep tones (note constant use of the same lick for the
D chord throughout)

VOCAL BACK-UP-- Begins with up-the-neck rolls, works down fingerboard to low tones, then moves up-the-neck to end.

MAY I SLEEP IN YOUR
BARN TONIGHT, MISTER?
KEY OF B♭

G tuning with the
5th string capo on
the 3rd fret of the
5th string.

Raise the pitch of the 5th string (to B♭) to sound like the 1st string at the 8th fret. Leave the other four strings in the open G tuning. [For practice: place your capo on the 4th fret and play the back-up for this tune along with the lead break (played open as written) for "She'll Be Comin' Around The Mountain" in the key of D.]

BANJO LEAD:

Primary chords = B♭, E♭, and F
I   IV   V

169

VOCAL BACK-UP--Roll patterns and passing tones on the deeper tones of the banjo:

MANDOLIN or
FIDDLE BACK-UP--Roll patterns and licks up-the-neck--providing a counter-melody for the fiddle:

170

VOCAL BACK-UP--up-the-neck rolls & licks--very active back-up:

171

DOBRO (OR GUITAR) BACK-UP--vamping and fill-in licks:

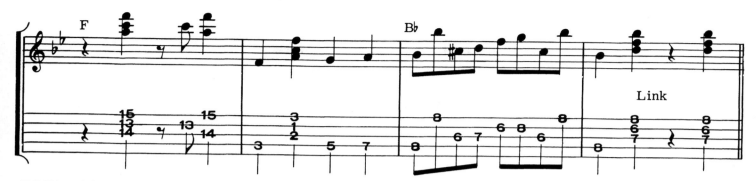

VOCAL BACK-UP--using up-the-neck rolls but less intense than for previous verse (winds down to end). (The back-up reaches a peak in the middle verse in this arrangement.)

WHEN THE SAINTS GO MARCHING IN
KEY OF F

(Primary chords = F, B♭, and C.)
I   IV   V

Do NOT retune your banjo or use the 5th string capo to play this arrangement. It is played in the open G tuning. [For Practice: place your capo on the 2nd fret so that the song is played in the key of G instead of F, and play the back-up along with the lead breaks for both "New River Train" and "Red River Valley". All three of these songs follow the same chord progression when they are played in the same key.]

BANJO LEAD:

VOCAL BACK-UP--Vamping: It is often safe, as well as effective to begin the back-up by vamping the chords to the song until you are familiar with the chord progression for the song.

For chorus (or refrain): Repeat vocal back-up (without pausing) and then begin fiddle back-up..

FIDDLE BACK-UP--played on the deeper tones of the banjo:

175

VOCAL BACK-UP--Using up-the-neck roll patterns:

Repeat vocal back-up for the refrain, then begin the dobro back-up.

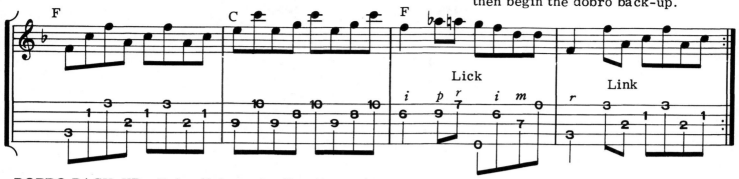

DOBRO BACK-UP--Using licks and roll patterns (notice that this arrangement uses many quarter notes (♩). This is common in back-up for dobro, guitar & harmonica.

177

VOCAL BACK-UP--using licks and roll patterns (up and down the fingerboard):

NOTE: For the verse: play the vocal back-up with the 1st ending (1.⌐——⌐)
For the refrain: Play the vocal back-up with the 2nd ending (2.⌐——⌐) [Skip the 1st ending]

SOLDIER'S JOY
C TUNING

Key of C

This is a traditional fiddle tune that is generally played in the Key of D. The banjo usually plays this tune in C Tuning, but with the capo placed on the 2nd fret. In this manner it can play along with the fiddle in the key of D. To tune the banjo to C tuning, lower the pitch of the 4th string the equivalent of two frets, to a C. (When the 4th string is fretted on the 7th fret, it should sound like the open 3rd string.) The same back-up techniques and patterns are used with this tuning, that are used with G tuning. The only difference is that the left hand should fret the 4th string two frets higher (in pitch) for the chords in C tuning, if the 4th string is to be picked by the right hand. (The low C chord leaves the 4th string open, however.)

LEAD BREAK:

179

SOLDIER'S JOY
BACK-UP

The songs, "Soldiers Joy", "Old Folks", and "Liberty" use exactly the same chord progression. Therefore, the following back-up arrangement can be used for any of these three songs.

BACK-UP: Using roll patterns on the deep tones of the banjo:(can be used as back-up
for any instrument--creates counter-melody in same tonal range with dobro or guitar and
counter balances the higher tones of the fiddle or mandolin)

NOTE: Vamping patterns can easily be used as back-up for this song by holding the chords in the same positions they are held for G tuning, but without using the 4th string when picking the patterns with the right hand.
NOTE: The only difference between C tuning and G tuning is that the 4th string is altered.

REUBEN
D TUNING-KEY OF D

Tune the 5th string to sound like the 1st string, 4th fret, (to F#);
Tune the 3rd string to sound like the 4th string, 4th fret, (to F#);
Tune the 2nd string to sound like the 4th string, 7th fret, (to A);
Leave the 1st & 4th strings alone, (both strings are D).

BANJO LEAD:

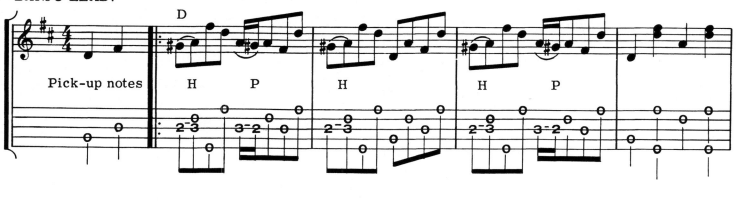

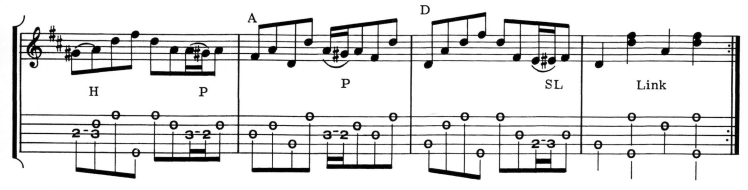

DOBRO (OR ANY INSTRUMENT) BACK-UP--Vamping chords:

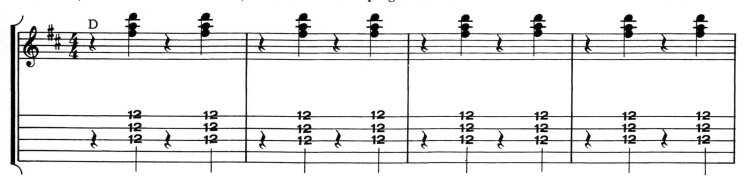

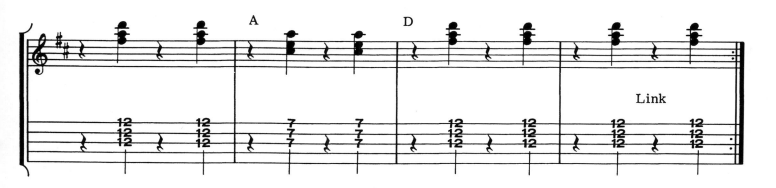

181

FIDDLE (OR ANY INSTRUMENT) BACK-UP--roll patterns on deep tones are effective back-up for any instrument. (The long D chord enables active back-up to compliment the lead.)

DOBRO OR GUITAR BACK-UP-- vamping variations and fill in licks (each vamp pattern=one measure)

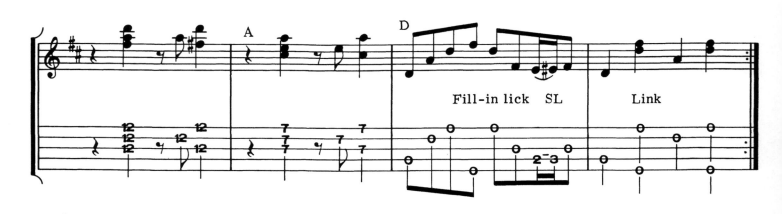

FIDDLE OR MANDOLIN BACK-UP-- deep tone roll patterns and using 7th chords for color:

DOBRO (OR ANY INSTRUMENT) BACK-UP--vamping and substitute chords:

* ALTERNATE(This syncopates the rhythm of measures 5 & 6 above)

NOTE: Any of the above arrangements can be used as vocal back-up.

FIDDLE TUNES

For many years, in the Appalachian Mountains, the banjo and the fiddle combination was considered a band. Earl Scruggs brought this tradition into the field of bluegrass music, and developed a style of accompaniment for the banjo to play along with the fiddle in a fiddle-banjo duet, without the presence of any other instrument. This style of back-up has evolved into a style of back-up which can be used for fiddle tunes when played by a full band by today's standards, as well as for the fiddle-banjo duets.

Because virtually every note played by the lead instrument in a fiddle tune is a melody note, the banjo's primary function is to provide rhythmic support along with a counter melody, which also provides harmonic support. To accomplish this, the left hand holds chord positions on the banjo, (or plays passing tones), while the right hand plays a note for almost every note played on the fiddle (or lead instrument).

The overall scheme of the banjo work consists primarily of back-up played on the deeper tones of the banjo. Fiddle tune back-up uses the same roll patterns, licks and passing tones discussed in the section on Scruggs-style back-up on the deep tones of the banjo, (see pp. 56-73) and also the fill-in licks on p. 28-9. (Generally, the standard roll patterns and their variations provide the basic rhythmic foundation for the back-up.) Also, at some point in the song, (often the B section of the melody), the banjo player usually slides into the upper region of the fingerboard and begins vamping chords to the rhythm of the song, using vamping patterns from pp. 16-19 (especially the basic pattern and pattern #1 from p. 19). This seems to add a surge of energy to the back-up and increases the overall tension and drive of the song. After several bars of vamping, the banjo returns to the deeper tones to close the song. If the fiddle plays several variations of the tune, the banjo may move briefly into the upper areas of the neck, but this usually functions as ornamentation of the lower tonal back-up, rather than as the primary area of back-up for the entire song. (i.e. Use licks from p. 98 or roll patterns.)

The songs on the following pages demonstrate how back-up can be played for several popular fiddle tunes. Typical of most fiddle tunes, the melody for each tune is divided into two parts, labeled Part A and Part B. (This should help you see how the vamping style can be used as back-up.) The songs also include several keys to demonstrate the fact that the back-up techniques are virtually the same, regardless of the key in which a song is played; only the chords are different.

NOTE: In the early fiddle banjo duets, the banjo player concentrated on playing a counter-melody to the fiddle by playing roll patterns according to the strongest primary chords to the song. As this style of back-up has developed into a general style of fiddle tune back-up to be used with complete bands, the musicians have added more chords to the accompaniment of many of these tunes by using chords which can be substituted for the primary chords. As a result, the back-up often involves playing two chords per measure of music, which necessitates dividing a roll in half between two chords so that each chord receives four notes, (i.e. Blackberry Blossom).

SALLY GOODIN'
KEY OF G

When playing this piece, the lead instrument often plays the tune several times in a row, (playing several variations of the melody), before relinquishing the lead to another instrument. The following back-up arrangements demonstrate how the banjo might accompany an instrument when it plays three variations in a row. (Play the lead break into a recorder three times without pausing, then play the back-up along with your recording.) The back-up arrangements are designed to demonstrate the rolls and licks which are commonly used as back-up for many different fiddle tunes played in the Key of G. (If the song is being played in another key, use the capo--i.e. Key of A = 2nd fret.) Although it is designated as fiddle back-up, the back-up can be used effectively to accompany almost any instrument playing this tune. (Generally the lead instrument plays a fiddle tune in the style of the fiddle.)

185

I.BACK-UP--using roll patterns & licks on deep tones of the banjo. (Each measure = one back-up pattern)

(Part A:)

(Part B:)

II. BACK-UP--begins with deep tones, then moves up-the-neck and changes to the vamping style:

(Part A:)

(Part B:)

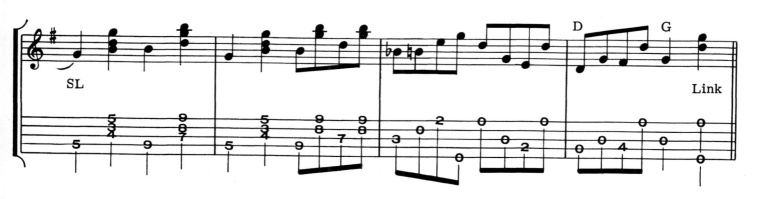

III. BACK-UP--Returns to deep tones:
(Part A:)

(Part B:)

ENDING--Repeat banjo break here or end song as follows. (without pausing):

GRAY EAGLE
KEY OF G

The chords in brackets [ ] are optional; these are substitute chords which have been added to the back-up in recent years. For practice: play the back-up for this tune along with the lead for "Sally Goodin'".

BANJO LEAD:

I. FIDDLE (or any instrument) BACK-UP--roll patterns on the deep tones of the banjo (creates counter melody):

(Part B:)

SL

SL SL Passing tones

Creating a counter-melody by playing
passing tones on the 4th string

II. FIDDLE (or any instrument) BACK-UP--the banjo becomes more active--increasing intensity of
the song:

(Part A)

...Up-the-neck embellishment...

returns to deep tones

SL

SL

(Part B)

FIDDLE (OR ANY INSTRUMENT) BACK-UP--vamping with substitute chords: (this style is very
III.   effective as guitar back-up)

(Part A:)

The right thumb creates a counter-melody by playing passing tones. (The substitute
chords act as passing chords leading the music from G to D.)

(Part B:)

191

IV.

FIDDLE (OR ANY INSTRUMENT) BACK-UP--using roll patterns with substitute chords:

(Part A)

(Part B)

BLACKBERRY BLOSSOM
KEY OF G

This tune demonstrates how back-up can be played for fiddle tunes which require frequent chord changes (i.e. two chords per measure).

BANJO LEAD:

I. FIDDLE BACK-UP--Roll patterns on the deep tones. (Due to 2 chords per measure, 4 notes = 1 chord and 4 notes = the other chord.)
(Part A:)

Each roll pattern is divided between two chords..

Mixed roll   Forward reverse   Forward-reverse roll

(Part B)

II.
FIDDLE (OR ANY INSTRUMENT) BACK-UP--counter-melody on 1st string--using MIMT pattern
(Mixed roll variation)
(Part A:)

(Part B:)

play em chord up-the-
neck-(embellishment).

III.

FIDDLE (OR ANY INSTRUMENT) BACK-UP--adding up-the-neck embellishment to II (above):

(Part A:)

(Part B:)

Forward roll.....
use left thumb ↓

Forward-reverse

IV.
FIDDLE BACK-UP--adding rhythmic embellishment (This is also effective as guitar or dobro back-up):
(Part A:)

Hold chords with left hand...

(Part B:)

H

COTTON PATCH RAG
KEY OF C

(G Tuning)

Note the similarity of the back-up for this tune to that of "Stone's Rag" in the Key of D.

BANJO LEAD:

(Part B:)

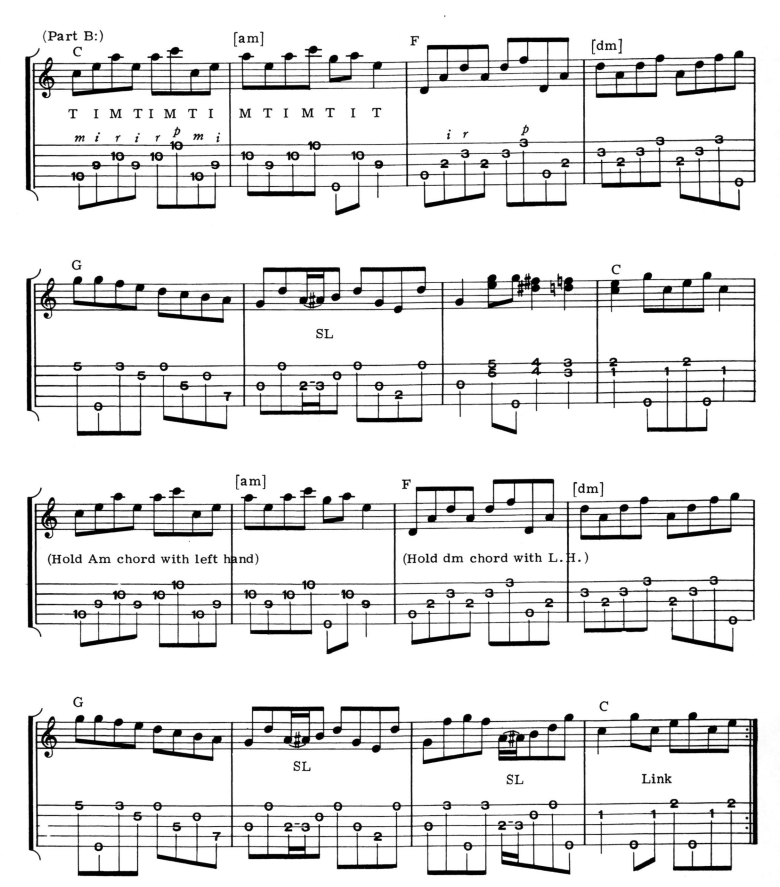

repeat lead (without pick-up notes), or begin playing back-up:

FIDDLE (OR ANY INSTRUMENT) BACK-UP--Part A uses roll patterns on deep tones: Part B vamps
chords up-the neck

(Part A:)

Common 2-measure back-up pattern used for
chords other than the open G chord.

SL
Common G chord back-up pattern

SL
Leads to "C"

...Common 2-measure pattern...

...2 measure pattern...

SL
G chord pattern

SL
Leads to "C"

(Part B:) (Each measure below contains a vamping pattern:)

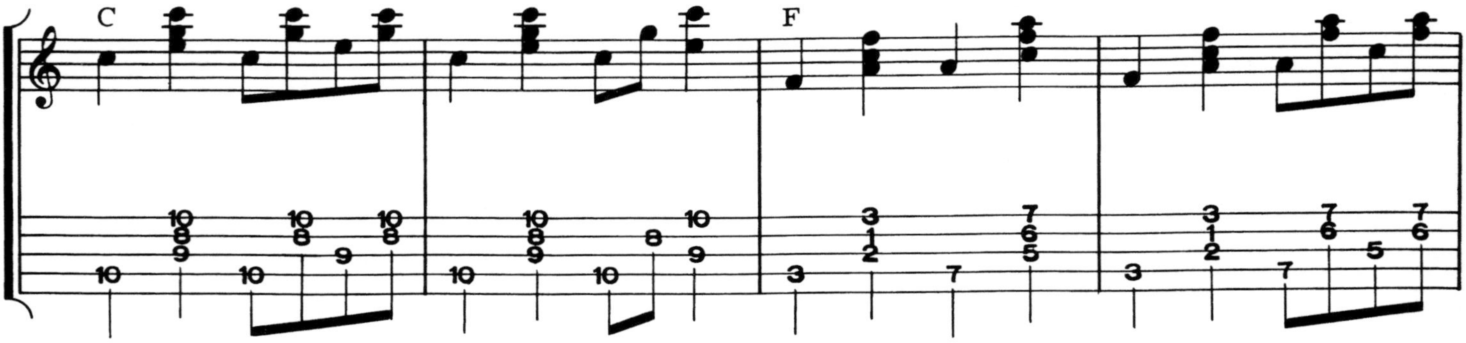

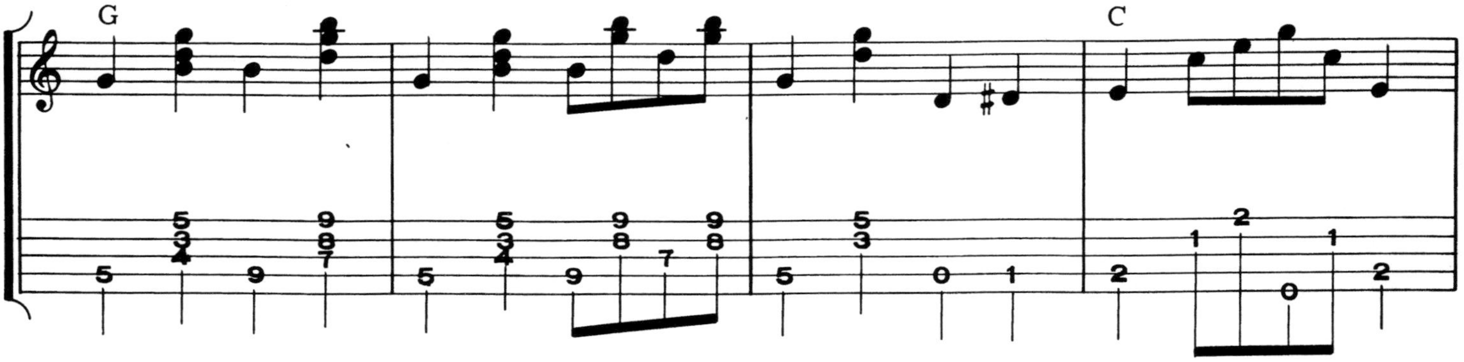

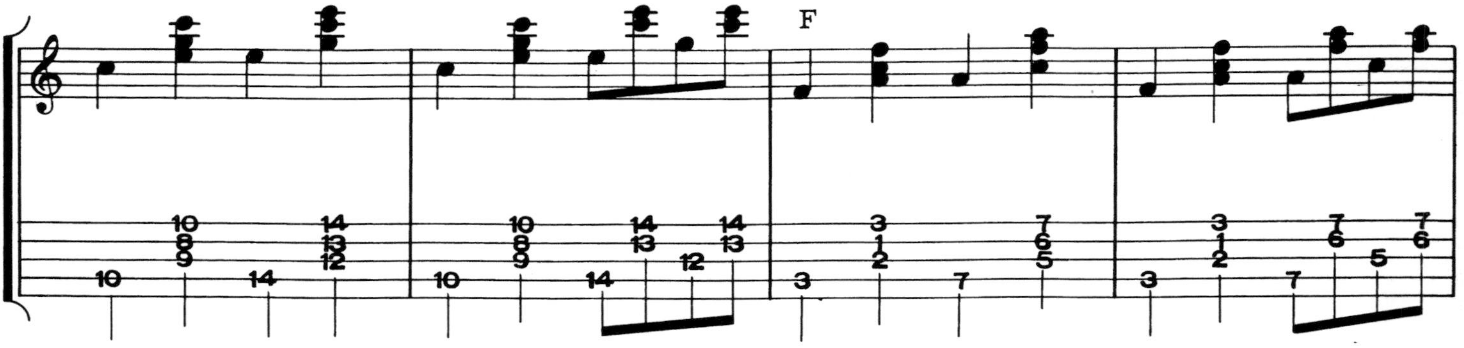

Closes with rolls on deep tones:

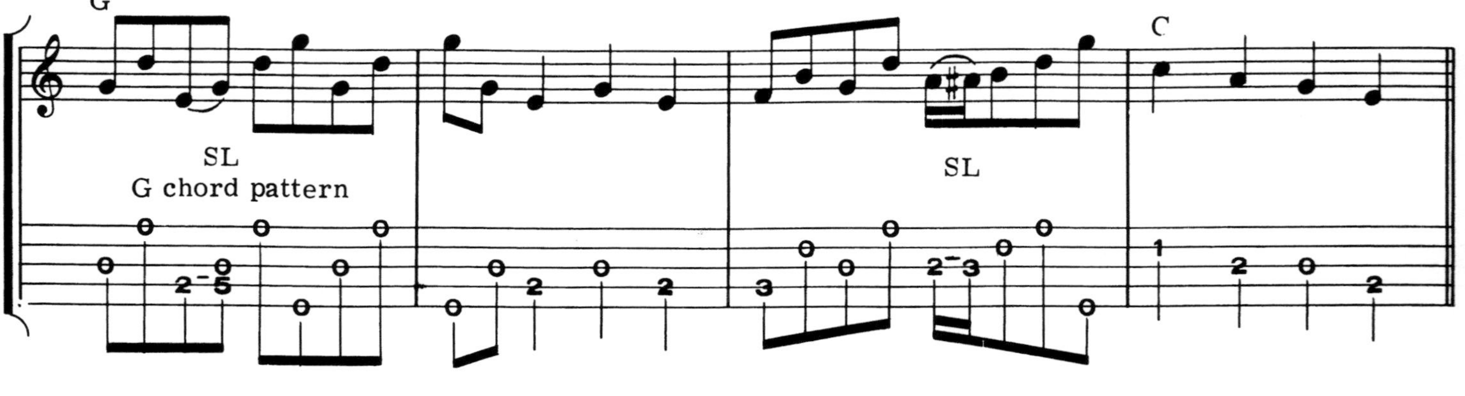

SL
G chord pattern

SL

STONE'S RAG
KEY OF D

G Tuning with 5th string
tuned to A (so that it is a
chord tone of the D chord).

Tune the 5th string (to A) to sound like the 1st string, 7th fret; (place the 5th string capo on
the 2nd fret;) (don't alter the other strings)

BANJO LEAD:

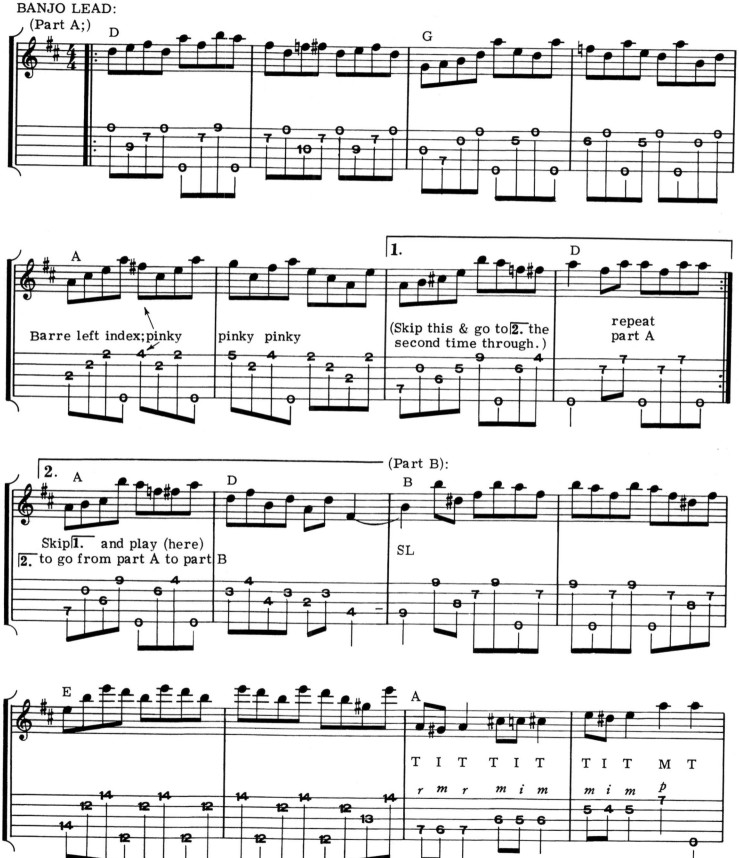

201

Repeat lead break or begin playing the back-up. (Don't pause)

FIDDLE (OR ANY INSTRUMENT) BACK-UP--using roll patterns for chords on deep tones for Part A; (Part A): vamping for part B:

Hold D chord with left hand...

... common 2 -

measure back-up pattern...

SLOW SONGS

Each of the right hand roll patterns used in Scruggs-style back-up for up tempo songs can be used effectively to accompany songs played at a slow tempo. The Mixed Roll pattern (alternating thumb) is often used to back-up slow songs when the back-up is played with the deeper tones of the banjo, and the Forward Roll is often used as the primary roll pattern for each chord in a song when the back-up is played with the higher tones of the banjo. Each pattern can be used as the sole rhythmic pattern throughout an entire song for every chord in the song, or it can be combined with the other back-up patterns appearing throughout this book, including the vamping patterns. Because these patterns have been covered in depth in previous pages, the information will not be repeated here. However, it is important to keep in mind that both the roll patterns and the vamping style of back-up are effective as back-up for slow songs.

Another type of right hand pattern has been frequently used to add a pleasant bounce to slower paced songs. This involves picking only two strings of the banjo with the right hand while holding partial chord positions with the left hand, generally in the middle or upper areas of the neck. Licks #9, #10, and #11 from the up-the-neck patterns, (page 95), are examples of this type of pattern. In addition to serving as embellishment to the roll patterns and other back-up licks, these patterns are frequently used as a STYLE of back-up for songs played at a slower tempo. The following patterns are examples of patterns which are frequently used with this style of back-up. Each pattern can be used as back-up for an entire song, or the patterns can be combined with one another to form the back-up. THE RIGHT HAND SHOULD BE POSITIONED IN THE "Y" POSITION--CLOSE TO THE AREA WHERE THE NECK JOINS THE HEAD OF THE BANJO--well away from the bridge! This style of back-up is effective for any instrumental lead break, but is generally preferred for vocal back-up. (See "Bury Me Beneath The Willow" (p.143) for an arrangement of a slow song to be played with several instruments.)

NOTE: In addition to the above styles of back-up for slow songs, a style of back-up based upon the playing of triplets can also be used. This will be covered under Waltz Time Back-up, (p.214). The techniques are the same, but in $\frac{3}{4}$ (waltz) time, each measure contains 3 triplets, whereas in the more common $\frac{4}{4}$ time signature, there are 4 triplets per measure. (All of the songs which have appeared in this book so far, are in $\frac{4}{4}$ time.)

Although written with 𝅘𝅥𝅮𝅘𝅥𝅮 for easy reading, the actual rhythm should be played as:
(stress the first note.)

Basic Right Hand Pattern

EACH PATTERN CAN BE PLAYED FOR ANY CHORD: (see chord progression p.206)
NOTE: THE LEFT HAND can hold PARTIAL CHORD POSITIONS, (the first two strings only), although it helps to think in terms of the full chord positions when locating each chord for the song.

1.

one measure

2.

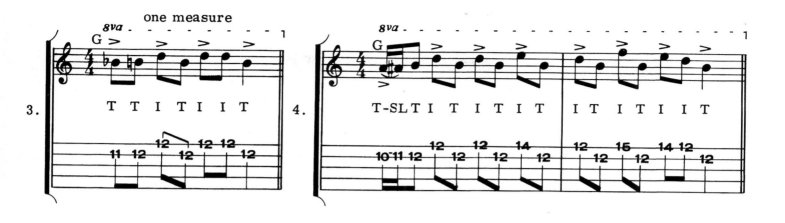

one measure

3.

4.

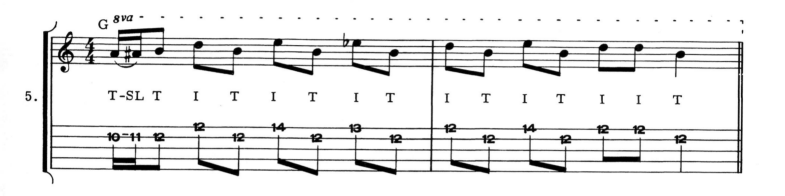

5.

Left hands travels from barre to "F" position

(Passing chord)

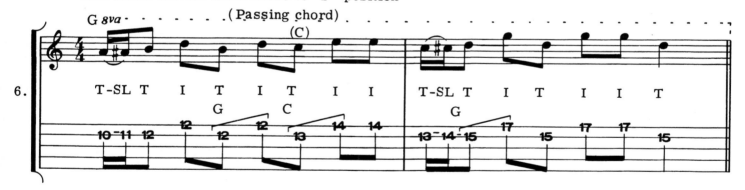

6.

Ending pattern

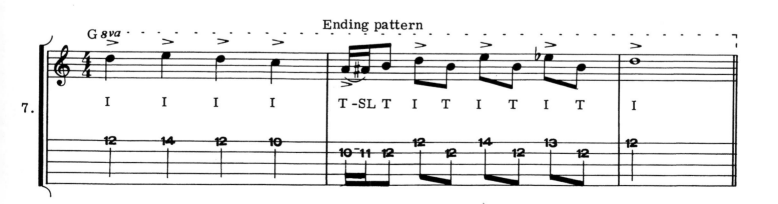

7.

One way to achieve a smooth harmony line is to move to the CLOSEST POSITION of the
next chord, in the direction you want the harmony to flow, (ascending or descending).

CHORD PROGRESSION
using slow song back-up pattern #1

WABASH CANNONBALL
BACK-UP

The following back-up arrangement uses lick #2 (on page 204) for each measure. Notice that the chords are played in the barre position.

NOTE: Accent the first note in each eighth note pair:

The following arrangement combines licks #1, #2, #7: (p.204-5) for back-up.

To end, play the first note (only) of the link. (The link can connect this back-up arrangement with any other back-up arrangement for this tune. (See pages: 33-38, 75, 101-106, 207 for other arrangements of this song.)

SWING LOW, SWEET CHARIOT

BACK-UP--ADDING PASSING TONES:

TOM DOOLEY

For additional practice, try playing roll patterns along with this lead.

LEAD:

BACK-UP--Using pattern #2 (p.204) for each chord in each measure:

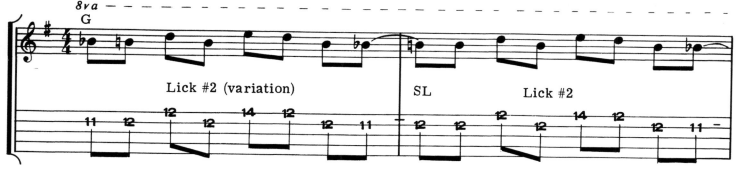

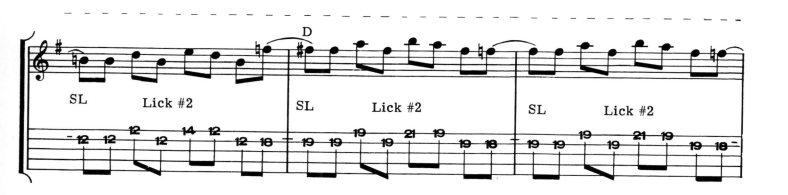

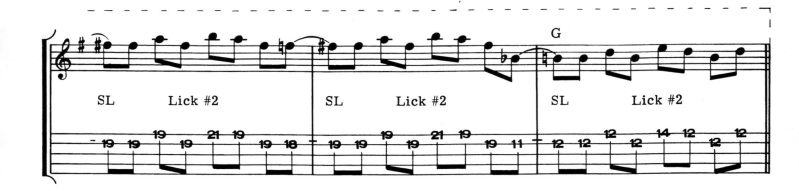

BACK-UP--Combining patterns (from pp. 204-6)

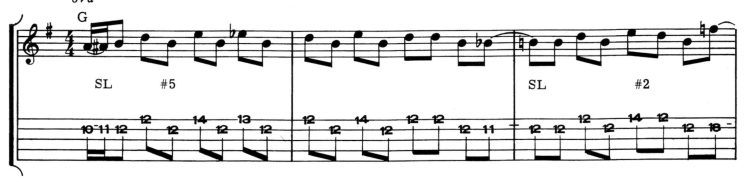

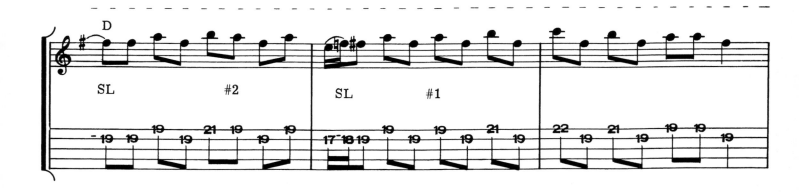

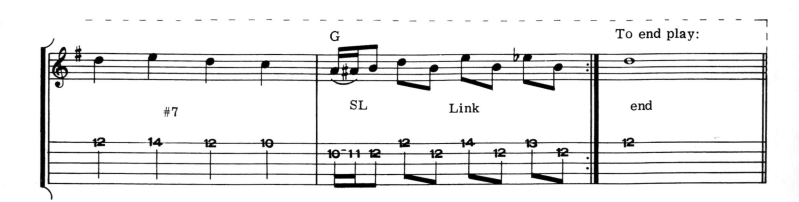

WALTZ TIME ($\frac{3}{4}$ TIME)

The following section is concerned with playing back-up for songs which are played or sung in a waltz rhythm, (in 3/4 time). Songs which are played in this dance rhythm have a pulse or rhythm pattern of three beats repeated over and over, with an accent or stress on the first beat. Often, the first indication that a song is being played in waltz time is when you just can't get a feeling for the song. If this occurs, stop for a minute and think:"ONE-two-three"along with the rhythm of the song. If a song is being played in waltz time, you should be able to "feel" the rhythm as: ONE-two-three-ONE-two-three-ONE-two-three-etc. Examples of songs played in this time signature are: "Blue Moon Of Kentucky" (slow part), "Tis Sweet To Be Remembered" (slow part), "Bouquet In Heaven", "Home On The Range", "I'll Be All Smiles Tonight", and many Christmas Carols, (i.e. "Silent Night").

All of the previously discussed styles of back-up can be easily adapted to 3/4 time. The essential difference is that for 3/4 time, you play in patterns of three beats, instead of the usual four beats. The following are the basic rhythm patterns used as back-up in waltz time. Each pattern can be played with the right hand while holding ANY chord with the left hand.

VAMPING PATTERNS:

213

ROLL PATTERNS: Each roll contains only six notes, instead of the usual eight notes.

4. Forward Roll: TIM TIM

5. Backward Roll: MIT MIT

6. Forward-Reverse Roll: TIMITM

7. Mixed Roll: TI TM TI

TRIPLETS: Each measure contains three triplets. (Accent the first note of each triplet.)

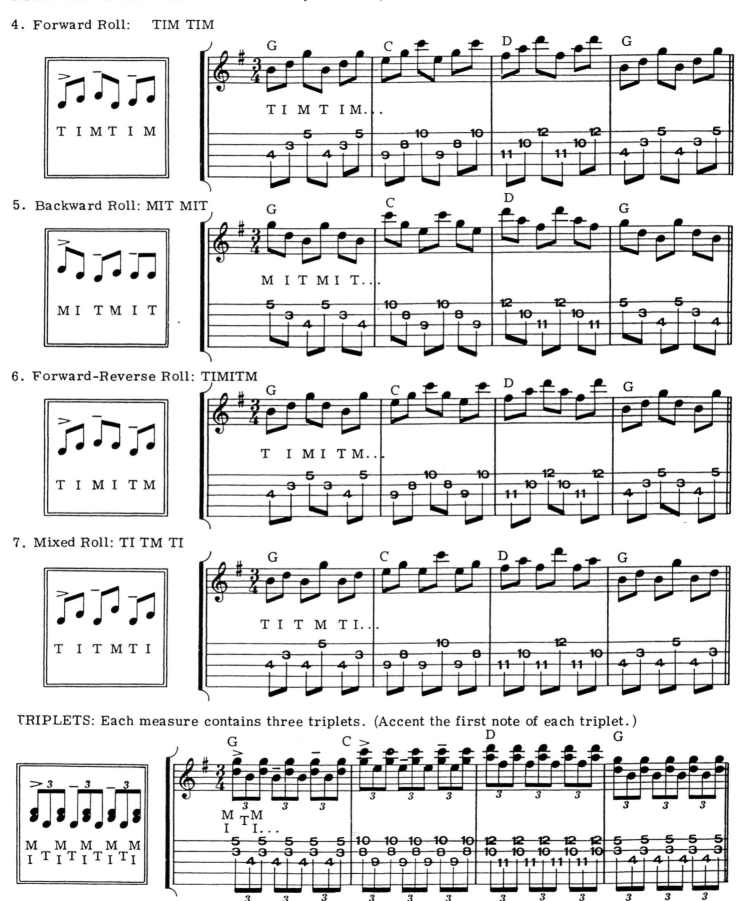

FILL-IN LICKS

The following lick patterns can be used to add interest to the back-up and to compliment the lead. Each lick is a pattern which can be applied to any chord.

"F" POSITION LICKS: The left hand works from the "F" position of the chord to play the following licks.

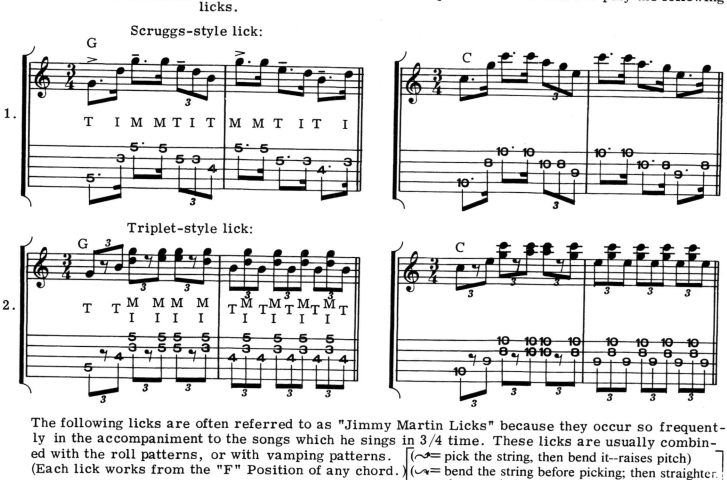

The following licks are often referred to as "Jimmy Martin Licks" because they occur so frequently in the accompaniment to the songs which he sings in 3/4 time. These licks are usually combined with the roll patterns, or with vamping patterns. [(~⤸= pick the string, then bend it--raises pitch) (⤵= bend the string before picking; then straighten. (Each lick works from the "F" Position of any chord.) --lowers pitch)]

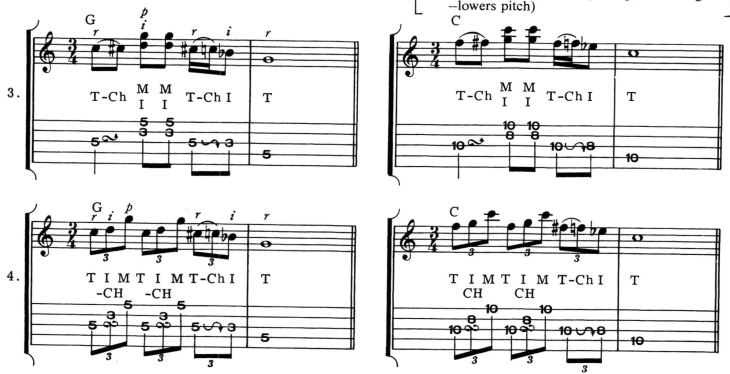

5.

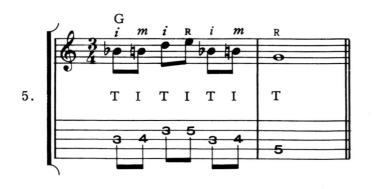

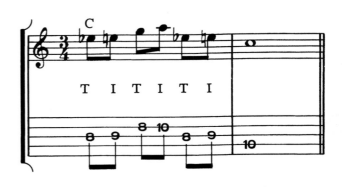

Barre L.H. fingers:

6.

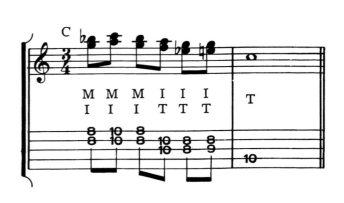

7.

(#8 can only be used for the G chord)

8.

CHORD PROGRESSION
Scruggs-style

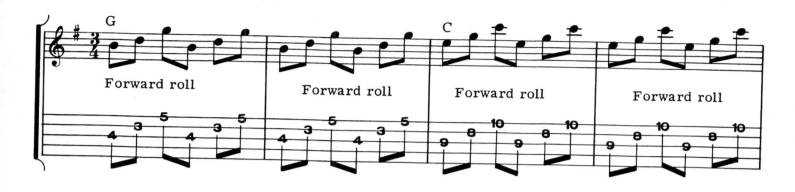

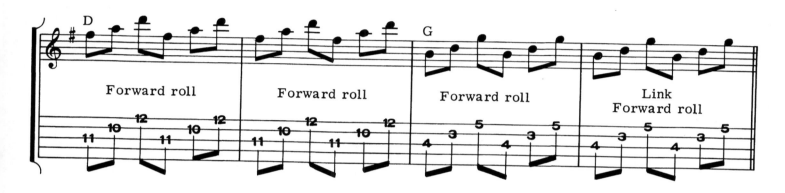

CHORD PROGRESSION
using "Jimmy Martin Licks"

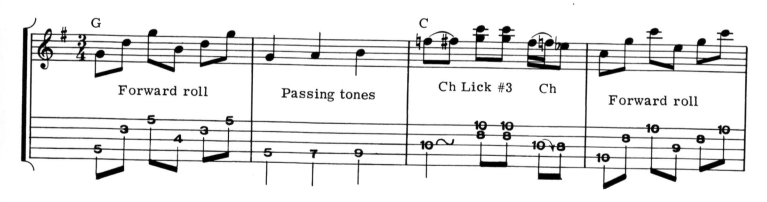

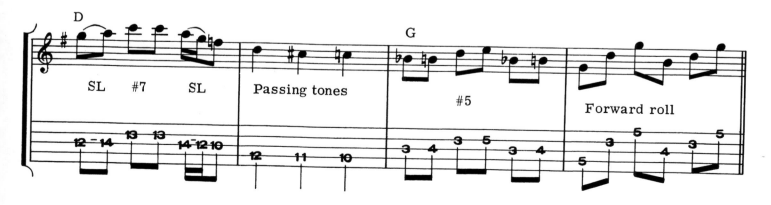

CHORD PROGRESSION
using triplets

ALL THE GOOD TIMES ARE PAST
LEAD

This is a very popular bluegrass song which is played in $\frac{3}{4}$ time. Each of the back-up arrangements for this song demonstrates a style of back-up which can be used to effectively accompany this tune. Although each arrangement can be used as back-up for any instrument, it is particularly effective for the instrument(s) noted above the arrangement.

<u>LEAD <u>ARRANGEMENT</u></u>:

NOTE: After playing the "Link," begin (any) back-up arrangement, (or repeat the lead break,) without pausing.

ALL THE GOOD TIMES ARE PAST
BACK-UP

I. VAMPING--Basic Pattern--Effective accompaniment for any instrument or for singing:

II. VAMPING --Adding passing tones and vamping pattern variations:

III. STANDARD ROLL PATTERNS ON DEEP TONES--vocal, fiddle, or mandolin backup:

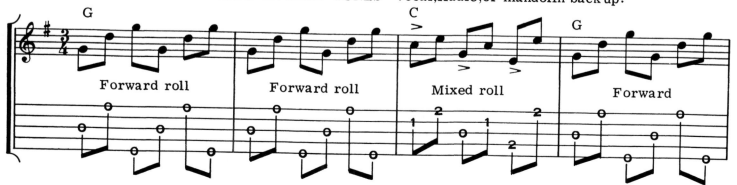

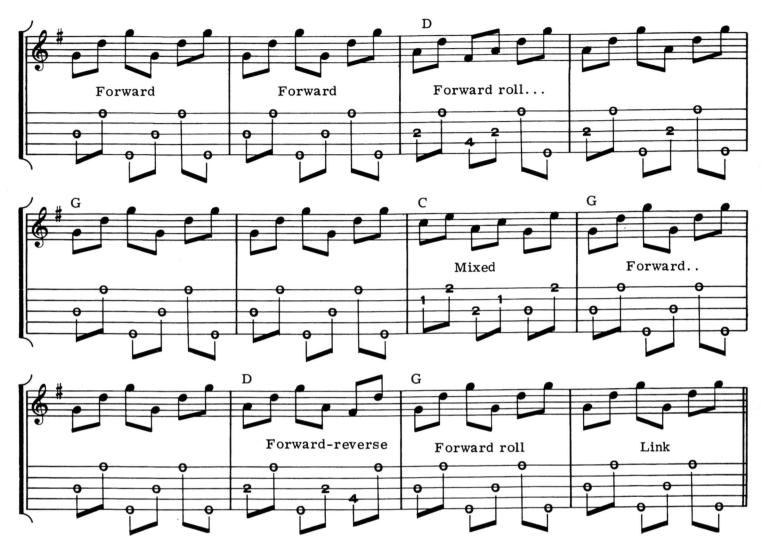

IV. Using roll pattern variations, passing tones, and fill-in licks: (Embellishing arr. III above)

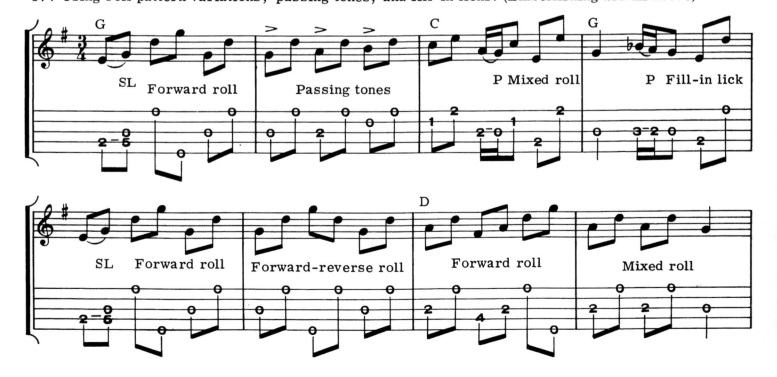

222

V. Using up-the neck roll patterns...vocal back-up:

223

VI. Adding fill-in licks.. Embellishing arr. V

224

VII. Using triplets: (Hold chords with left hand throughout)-vocal back-up

225

VIII. Adding passing chords:

226

IX. Triplets using full chords, passing chords, & fill-in licks: (Pause for the 𝄾 in ♪ 𝄾 ♪)

DOWN IN THE VALLEY

Following the lead break establishing the melody, are several back up arrangements which can be used to accompany this tune.

I. BACK-UP: I. Vamping--effective back-up for any instrument or for singing--

II. VAMPING--Adding passing tones and vamping pattern variations:

III. Roll Patterns with deep tones--effective as fiddle, mandolin, & vocal back-up:

229

IV. Adding Passing Tones and Left-Hand Techniques (slides, pull-offs, etc):

V. Embellishment by picking same string twice with Right Hand -- (Adds bounce)--effective as vocal back-up (hold chord with L.H.):

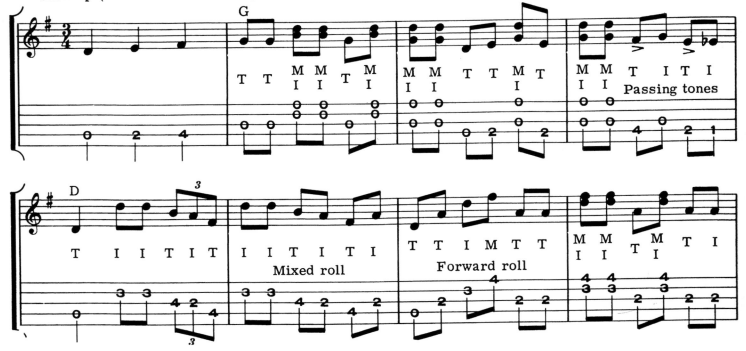

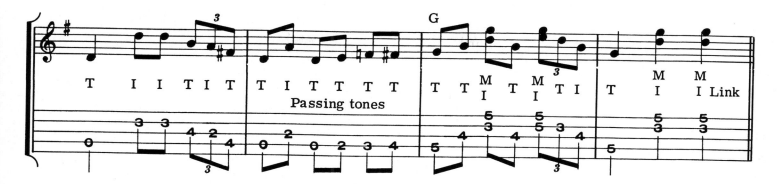

VI. Up-The-Neck Roll Patterns--effective as vocal back-up (also works for guitar & dobro back-up):

VII. Adding Fill-In Licks To Up-The-Neck Roll Patterns -- Vocal back-up:

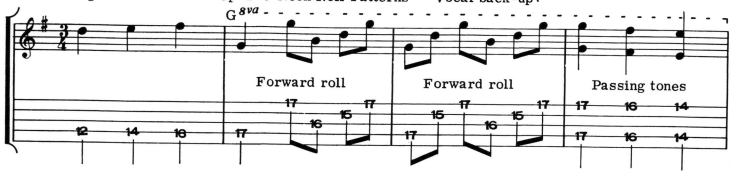

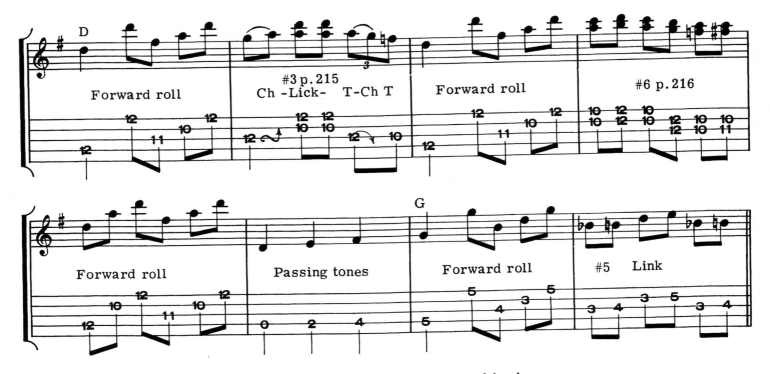

VIII. Using Triplets--Hold chords with left hand--effective vocal back-up:

CURRENT TRENDS IN BACK-UP

Once you have mastered the styles of back-up and the basic back-up techniques discussed throughout this book, there are several avenues you can travel to continue improving your skills for playing accompaniment. The majority of professional banjo players today use the "Vamping Style" of back-up and the "Scruggs-Style" back-up patterns as the basis of their back-up. In addition to the standard back-up patterns, licks are being extracted from lead breaks for use as back-up patterns for specific chords. Also, more and more emphasis is being placed upon the expansion of the basic parameters of music. New rhythm patterns which employ a great deal of syncopation are being explored, for use within the roll patterns and licks, as well as within the vamping style of back-up. Chords are being expanded, both for color, (i.e. added tones forming 6th chords, 7ths, 9ths, etc.) and also for function, (i.e. to lead the music to new chords). Passing chords are replacing passing tones in many instances to emphasize chord changes, (through the use of substitute chords). Also, substitute chords are often used to serve the function of primary chords in a song, (i.e. the relative minor chord is often used in place of a Major chord). Substitute chords are also becoming more and more an integral part of the harmony of fiddle tunes. (For possible uses of chords as Substitute Chords, see the Chord Charts on the following pages, under the discussions for Advanced Back-up.)

Scales are also being used as back-up patterns according to the chords in songs. There is a style of back-up which is based upon the use of various chromatic and diatonic scale patterns; however, because this style is so active, most banjo players do not use it as a style of back-up for an entire song, but instead, employ some of the scales, and the licks based upon the scales, within the context of Scruggs-style back-up, particularly to guide the ear of the listener to new chords, (i.e. a D scale w/flat 7th leads the music from a D chord to a G chord, ("D" mixolydian mode).

Several styles of back-up have also emerged which can be used for slow songs. These styles utilize the theory of "Harmonic Rhythm", which states that the slower a song is played, the greater the number of chords the accompaniment is able to play per measure of music. One of the most popular styles of back-up utilizing this theory, is often referred to as the "Triplet Style" of back-up, (see "Waltz Time Back-Up). Scale patterns are frequently used with this style of back-up, both to lead the music to new chords, and as embellishment, while the triplet rhythm is used to provide a full harmony for the chords to the song. Several licks have also been developed for this style of back-up, which are now used by many banjo players.

The above suggestions are only a few of the possible areas of back-up which a person can study to improve his skills for playing accompaniment. However, almost every "good" (effective) banjo player first masters the styles of back-up discussed in this book. They, in themselves, provide effective back-up for many different songs, and once mastered, provide an excellent foundation upon which to build, and from which to expand.

CHORD CHART-G TUNING
MAJOR CHORDS

Major chords are formed from the 1st, 3rd, & 5th tones of the major scale of the chord name. There are three left hand positions for all of the major chords. (see p.10)

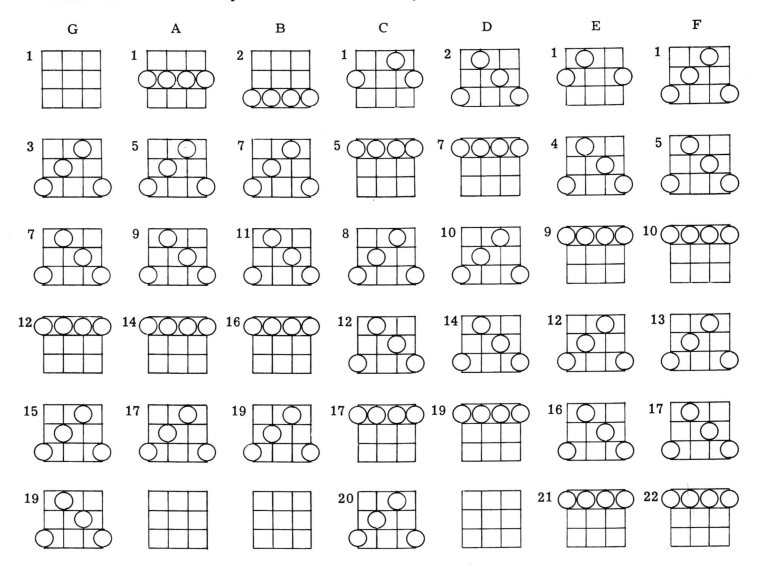

The number by each individual diagram tells you what fret the chord starts on. (NOTE: For ♯ &♭ chords, see p.14)

FOR ADVANCED BACK-UP:

Major chords provide the primary chords for songs played in major keys. (Most bluegrass songs fall into this category.) In addition, they can also be substituted for other chords in a song, either to fulfill the function of that chord, or to add color to the back-up. For example, a major chord can:

1.) Be used as a lower neighbor chord for color, (play the chord 2 (or 1) frets lower than the chord it is being substituted for). i.e. for G, play F, (or G-F-G)
2.) Be used as a passing chord to lead the music from one chord to another.
3.) Be substituted for its relative minor (or its secondary minor), (for a minor chord 2 letters before (or after) the chord name in the alphabet--i.e. G for em;C for am; D for bm.)
4.) Substitute as the ♭V chord of any chord--i.e. substitute A♭ for D; D♭ for G; (This works nicely for a V-I progression--ie. instead of playing D to G, play A♭ (for D) to G.)

MINOR CHORDS
(SYMBOL = m)

A minor chord is formed by flatting the 3rd of the major chord of the same name. There are three left hand positions for all of the minor chords. (see p.14)

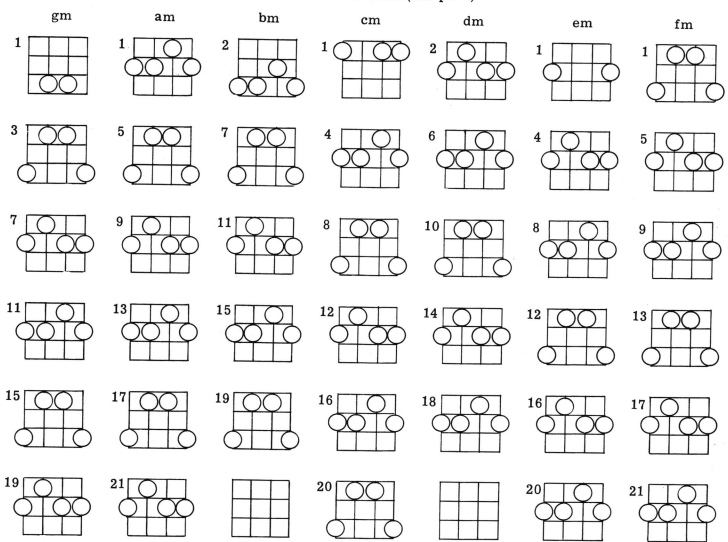

The number by each individual diagram tells you what fret the chord starts on. (Minor chords are usually indicated with small letters.)

FOR ADVANCED BACK-UP:

Minor chords are frequently used in back-up as substitute chords. For example:
1. Substitute a minor chord for its relative major chord. i.e. for G play em; for C play am; for D play bm. This adds color to the back-up.
2. Substitute the secondary minor chord for its major chord. i.e. for G play bm; for C play em; for D play f♯m. (The minor chord located a major 3rd higher)
3. Substitute the parallel minor for its major chord in a IV-I progression. i.e. for C to G play cm to G, (or C-cm-G); for G-D, play gm-D.
4. Substitute the minor ii chord for the major V chord. i.e. for V-I play ii-I; for D to G play am to G instead; for G to C play dm to C instead.
5. Minor chords are often used as passing chords. i.e. for a V→I chord change, play V-IV-iii-ii I. (The first four chords are played for the V chord.) For ex.: play D-C-bm-am (for D) then G; play G-F-em-dm-to go to C. Also: as passing chords for I-IV substitute iii-♭iii-ii→(for I)-then play IV. i.e. to go from G to C play em-e♭m-dm (for G) then C. (Many times in the key of G, the link between a verse & chorus can use this. Also: for I-IV you can play I-ii-iii→IV. (i.e. G-am - bm→C, for G to C)

DIMINISHED CHORDS
(SYMBOL = O)

The diminished chord is formed by flatting the 3rd and the 5th of the major chord. Although the diminished chord can be formed by the left hand in several different positions, more commonly, the ♭7th is added to the chord, so that the same fingering position on the banjo can be used to play several diminished chords of different names. The following are the most popular diminished chord positions. (Each position can be played three frets higher for the same chords.)

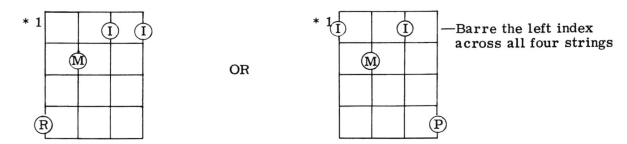

When the lowest tones of these positions are held on the:

* 1st fret, the chord is f#°, a°, c°, e♭°, g♭°, and d#°. (Any of these.) The same position begun on any of the following frets will also result in the above chords: 4th, 7th, 10th, 13th, 16th, 19th.

2nd fret, the chord is g°, b♭°, d♭°, f♭°, e°, a#°, and c#°. The same position begun on any of the following frets will also result in the above chords: 5th, 8th, 11th, 14th, 17th, 20th.

3rd fret, the chord is g#°, b°, d°, f°, a♭°, and c♭°. These chords can also be played at the 6th, 9th, 12th, 15th, 18th, 21st frets.

FOR ADVANCED BACK-UP:

All of the tones in a fully diminished 7th chord are located a minor 3rd apart. Due to the equidistance of the intervals, this chord can be resolved in four directions, (each tone leads to a different chord). Because this chord is so unstable it has many uses in back-up, both for color and for function. For example:

1. As a passing chord--play the diminished position of the vii chord of the major chord you are changing to. i.e. play f#° then G; or C#° then D. (The passing chord is played while the song is on the chord you are changing from.)

2. As a substitute chord for V (Substitute vii° for V). i.e. substitute f#° for D; b°for G. This is particularly useful when going from V-I. For example, for D to G, play f#° instead of D, then play the G chord.

3. In a IV to I progression, iv°or i°can be used as a passing chord. i.e. C to c° to G instead of simply C to G; or C to g° to G instead of simply C to G.

4. Diminished chords are useful as pivot chords to achieve quick modulations into remote keys.

AUGMENTED CHORDS
(SYMBOL = +)

An augmented chord is formed by raising the 5th of the major chord of the same name. The left hand fingering position is the <u>same</u> for all augmented chords. (see p. 14 also).

The number by each individual diagram indicates the fret the chord starts on.

FOR ADVANCED BACK-UP:

Augmented chords are frequently used as substitute chords to lead the ear of the listener into a new chord. For example:
1. When going from the V chord back to the I chord, play the V+ chord instead of the major V chord. i.e. instead of playing D then G, play D+ then G.
2. Augment the I chord before going to the IV chord. i.e. in the Key of G, play G+ to go to C, rather than the regular (major) G chord.
3. Augmented chords are frequently substituted for 7th chords.

DOMINANT SEVENTH CHORDS
(SYMBOL = 7)

A dominant 7th chord is formed by adding the flat 7th tone of the major scale of the chord name, to the major chord.

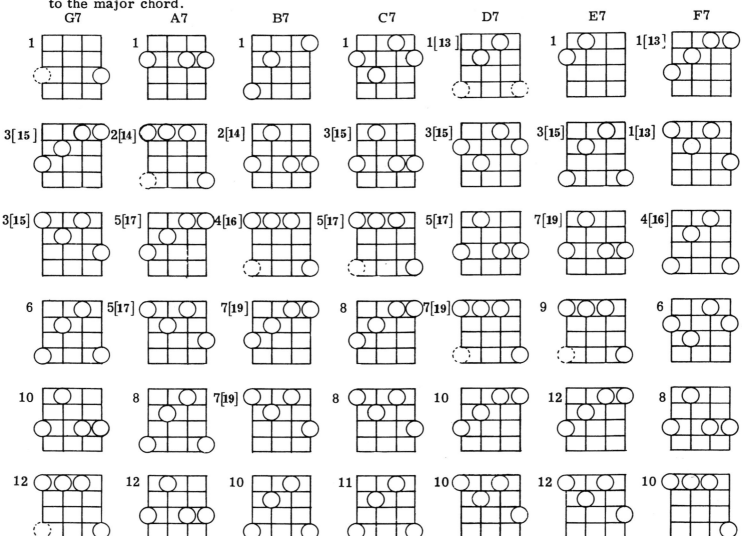

The number by each individual diagram tells you what fret the chord starts on. (Two numbers by a diagram indicate two different locations.) ( ) = optional

FOR ADVANCED BACK-UP:

Seventh chords are frequently used in back-up to add color to the back-up, and also to lead the music into new chords. For example:

1. The most common use of the 7th chord is to substitute the V7 chord for V when the I chord follows. i.e. play D7 (instead of simply D) to lead the ear to the G chord; play G7 to go to C; play A7 to go to D.
2. Seventh chords are frequently used to embellish the back-up--especially when the back-up is played with the higher pitched tones of the banjo. i.e. simply play G7 instead of G; C7 instead of C, etc.
3. The 7th can be added to any type of chord, although the above chart is only for the dominant (flat) 7th chord. i.e. gm can also be gm7.

NOTE FOR BEGINNERS: The basic form of a 7th chord can easily be substituted for the 7th chord, if you can't find the chord position for the 7th. i.e. simply play G for G7; gm for gm7: etc.

Everybody's Music Teacher